"This book will definitely help me in raising my two-year-old twins. I enjoyed the humor, and the examples throughout the book were great! I thought the book was funny and easy to read."

—Tara Smith (mother of two)

"My grandson was free of temper tantrums within two weeks after my daughter and I attended Leanna's tantrum seminar. It works."

—Georgia Haynes (retired English teacher)

"Leanna's solutions ring true. Her 'secret' is a simple, doable concept that can have powerful results and make you feel good about your parenting and your relationship with your children."

—Angela Larson (mother, grandmother, business owner, member of Soroptimist International)

"I was an extremely defiant child, but, through all the years my mother and I struggled over who was going to be in charge, I always *loved* how she responded to my anger."

—(child of Leanna Rae Scott)

MegaMom's Wisdom™ For Tantrums

The Tantrum Book to End All Tantrums™

The Secret to Total Prevention and Total
Elimination of Temper Tantrums:
Infant Anger Management™

Leanna Rae Scott

MegaMom™ Media, Salt Lake City

MegaMom's Wisdom for Tantrums
The Tantrum Book to End All Tantrums
The Secret to Total Prevention and Total Elimination of
Temper Tantrums: Infant Anger Management

First edition copyright ©2010 Leanna Rae Scott

For permission requests, address
info@megamommedia.com

ISBN: 978-0-9823317-1-2

Published by MegaMom Media, Salt Lake City

Design and layout by MegaMom Media™

Cover design by Ira Tiffen

Author photograph by Judy M. G. McDonald

Copy editing by Tara Smith

Acknowledgments

I would like to thank each and every person throughout the past thirty-some years that encouraged me to write this book. I would also like to thank the many people who gave me feedback as I wrote it. Some people gave me very extensive feedback, including much constructive criticism, which I appreciate. (Thankfully, that was the only kind of criticism I personally received.)

I would like to thank my thirteen children and my step-daughter for their positive influence and for being the delightful, loveable people with whom I got to learn all this stuff on. (I would also like to apologize to them, formally and in print, for any and all of my actual and/or perceived parental failings.)

I would like to thank my first two exes for their genetic contribution to the existence of these wonderful offspring.

I want to thank my oldest son and my daughter-in-law for their extensive and excellent help and advice with this book.

I am truly grateful for the exceptional, constant, and devoted help of my husband, without whom I'd be writing these acknowledgments at least a year or two later than right now and without whom the sweetness of these moments would certainly be much less intense.

I would like to officially apologize to a whole generation of temper-tantrum parents who did without my secret of eliminating temper tantrums (while I withheld it for thirty-three years of preparing to write this book). In my defense, I just want to say that I verbally gave each and every person my secret when they asked for it.

Dedication

I would like to dedicate this book to all of my children (who have given me the greatest satisfaction in my life) and to Ira (the man I would have made every effort to have in my life from my parenting debut, had I only known what I know now).

Table of Contents

Chapter One: An Introduction; Who Am *I* To Be Telling *You* About *Temper Tantrums*?

This is the part of the book where I briefly let you know what perspective I'm coming from, how my biases originated, what my lifestyle has been, and what my attitudes are. I realize this is not exactly essential in your understanding of the concepts I teach about temper tantrums, but I believe in being explicit about my biases. Besides—my lifestyle has been unusual enough that numerous people, including total strangers, have for many years expressed much curiosity about it. So, to give you a sense of what I'm all about, I will share some details about myself.

I am mother to thirteen children (six sons and seven daughters), step-mother to another daughter, and currently grandmother to forty-eight grandchildren and step-grandchildren. I gave birth to ten children in my first marriage of seventeen years and three in my second marriage of eight years.

I've been divorced three times. Most of my parenting experience—thirty-two years of it—was of the pseudo-single-parenting variety because my first three spouses unfortunately turned out to be mostly non-participating parenting partners. Also, I did actually single-parent for a total of eight years. But I'm finally, at the tail end of my parenting career, experiencing a delightful, egalitarian co-parenting marriage.

For the first twenty years or so of raising my family, I mostly was a stay-at-home mom. However, I did operate and assist with quite a number of small business ventures, including many years of teaching accounting to small business owners, and four years of performing in and promoting

1

our family country music band with my first husband and ten children.

I taught my kids to share in the household chores, gardening, canning, freezing, baking, cooking, and yard work. My priority right from the early parenting years was becoming the best mother I could be, and I regularly accessed parenting advice in books and seminars. During my pregnancy years, I put on hold my long-time dream of writing books because I first wanted to make time to get more education.

At the end of my second marriage, I accelerated from part-time to full-time university courses that I was taking by distance. It took me fifteen years, on and off, to obtain a bachelor's degree, with distinction (double majors in psychology and women's studies). Also, during those fifteen years, I earned a Counseling Women Certificate and completed a Small Business Management Program and a Telephone Crisis Counseling Training program.

I worked at various places, including as a crisis counselor and social worker at a women's shelter, a case manager in a counseling agency, a customer service agent (including at an airline), and as a self-employed copyeditor. I did much of this while single-parenting seven or more children, for sixteen months also single-foster-parenting four children, and while providing regular voluntary advocacy and life coaching services to dozens of individuals. I have since completed my hours towards my SSW social work license by working as an activities specialist and teen-mothers' advocate at a women's shelter. I currently have one child living at home (age nineteen).

The first big goal in my life was to have *a lot* of children. I pursued that goal like I have every other one before and since—to the hilt. My primary, most honest way of explaining this atypical goal is to say that, in general, I don't do much in moderation. That's just who I am.

Another one of my traits is that I love to share anecdotes, and this just happens to be an anecdote moment. One time, way back when I only had seven children, and I was out shopping with all of them, a woman that I'd noticed observing me from a distance came up to me and asked, "Are these kids all yours?" (Of course, that wasn't an uncommon thing for me to be asked—but this questioner was different.) After I admitted that the kids were all mine, this woman started circling me, looking me up and down, and studying me. After her second or third trip around me, she loudly stated for the whole store to hear, "I don't believe it!"

I waited for this woman to do the typical follow up with what it was she didn't believe—maybe that I didn't look like I'd had that many children, or that I didn't look old enough to have seven kids, or that I still had a waistline, or some such thing. But she didn't say anything like that. She just kept shaking her head, exclaiming, "I don't believe it! I don't believe it!"

By then we had quite an audience, and I was getting a little embarrassed, so I outright asked her, "*What* don't you believe?"

That's when she said, "I don't believe it. *You actually look sane!*"

I'm under absolutely no illusion whatsoever that every one reading my work thinks well of me for having and raising thirteen children. Seriously, people have been disabusing me of that naïve notion for decades. Many times I've been reprimanded in public by total strangers, somewhat like fur-coat wearers have often been scolded by animal-rights activists—with the bucket of paint splashed all over the coat—Whoosh! "Take that, you animal killer, you!"

Not that I think there's an *official* organization of anti-prolific-parents activists. I probably just occasionally and accidentally ran into people who disapproved of my lifestyle and who weren't opposed to publicly scolding me. Actually, it was more like *they* ran into *me*. For sure, I was an extremely easy target for them when I had my brood with me.

I didn't, of course, get any buckets of paint from these overpopulation theorists. But I got "buckets" of disapproving comments—Whoosh! "You baby maker! How dare you overpopulate my world! How dare you produce so many children that you couldn't possibly look after them all properly! Look at them! Not one of them has designer jeans! And that one even has a patch! Oh my word!"

Or sometimes it was people in my community— Whoosh! "How dare you have ten children and be thinner than me with only two! How dare you provoke my husband into pointing this fact out to me!—every week!—for the past year!—and twice on Mother's Day!" Of course, not every one who would have liked to scold me in that way actually did. Most of them just gave me "buckets" of attitude.

I understand that we don't all have the same views and beliefs about the ideal family size. But we don't have to. If you've decided to only have one or two children (or none), more power to you. You won't get any disapproval from me. I trust that those of you who do take issue with my "mass" reproduction will be able to put that aside enough to be able to benefit from what I have to share about Infant Anger Management, discipline methods, and temper tantrums.

My methods work with children as individuals and have absolutely nothing to do with family size.

No matter what people's perspectives on large families, their initial reactions are pretty much identical when they first hear how many kids I have. (That is, after they ask me between one and five times—depending maybe on how gullible they fear themselves to be—if I am serious.)

People's reactions usually begin with Stage One where, in shock, their jaws drop open wide enough for wisdom-tooth repair. Typically, in Stage Two their jaws drop even a little wider and remain agape while the two of us make lengthy eye contact. I observe their facial expressions that indicate the formation of thoughts, comments, or questions while I try to guess (based on the amount of horror in their expressions) whether they will be pro or con. I patiently wait for them to eventually regain their composure.

Upon jaw closure, most people throw a few personal questions at me, temporarily forgetting everything their mothers taught them about manners. Usually the first point-blank question (especially from men) is, "How *old* are you?"

Women sometimes remember to add, "*If* you don't mind me asking" before *expecting* me to answer. After years of such discourtesy I eventually decided to make people guess my age before I answered them. In doing so, they often guessed me quite a bit older than I was—because (they explained in embarrassment) of how many kids I had.

I know that some of my readers are also likely wondering a few things about my experience of raising so many children, so I might just as well go ahead and answer some of those questions before I move on to the temper tantrum part of the book. Here are my answers:

- Yes, I really did *actually* have thirteen children.
- Yes, which I physically gave birth to.
- Yes, from my very own uterus.
- Yes, all vaginal deliveries.
- No, no twins or triplets.
- No, I did not *love* being pregnant.
- No, I did not have *easy* pregnancies.

5

- Yes, we often did have a big house.
- Actually, I *can't* tell you how *I* did it all because I *didn't* do it all by myself. The kids helped with the mountain of work and we functioned as a team.
- Yes, it did cost a lot of money, but we compensated by living frugally and saving a lot of money by growing, cooking, and preserving food; sewing and mending clothing; shopping wisely; and many, many other things. (I worked sixteen hours a day seven days a week for more than thirty-five years.)
- Yes, I do tend to be very organized, but I have also learned to tolerate a high degree of chaos.
- Yes, Christmases have been fun.
- No, in *fact*, we *did* own a television, heh, heh, heh. But after the first four kids or so, I didn't have a *whole* lot of time to watch it.
- Au contraire. We *were* smart enough to figure out what was causing it—many years, in fact, before we were old enough to "join the cause" of procreation.
- Yes *indeed*, we *had* heard of birth control. And believe it or not, we actually used it to space our children—an average of twenty-three months apart over a twenty-three-year period. My oldest is forty-one, and my youngest is eighteen.

My first five children all threw temper tantrums as babies ... my last eight didn't. My fifth child, at the age of fourteen months, was free of tantrums within a week or so after I figured out what to change in my parenting style. That was thirty-three years ago.

I gave birth to my first child two months before I turned eighteen. (Doesn't that sound tons better than, "I had my first child when I was seventeen"?—another event that total strangers feel the right to condemn a mother for, even if she felt very ready, happy, eager, and prepared for the experience at that age.)

When my first child started throwing temper tantrums more than forty years ago, I consulted with more experienced parents around me, and I started accessing parenting advice in books and magazines—none of which helped me in any way to prevent the tantrums. So I carried on until I stumbled onto the answer with my fifth child. After that, I tested out and continually improved upon my theories while I had and raised eight more children along with the others.

For decades now I have been privately sharing my tantrum insight with self-designated needy parents (with or without bended knee and without the often proffered payment for the verbal pre-book version of my advice). But I'm now ready, after agonizingly lengthy preparations, to formally share my learning on this subject.

I hope you will gain what you need and want from this description of my temper tantrum elimination and prevention method, which I call *Infant Anger Management*. I also hope you know and are expecting that the content of this book is entirely geared to eliminating and preventing *only* the temper tantrums of babies and children—because I have absolutely no clue whatsoever how to prevent temper tantrums in husbands. So I can't help you with that, and I hope that's not what you were expecting—wait, I'm just kidding—I actually do have lots of expertise with adult anger management, but that's for another book.

Also, I'm not going to concentrate on anger management techniques for teenagers in this book. That information, too, will be under a separate cover. This is mostly because teens generally suffer from what I call *Pre Adult Syndrome (or PAS)*, not entirely unlike PMS, both of which seem to be hormonally driven states that often involve symptoms of irrationality and super-emotionality. Teen Anger Management assistance often involves additional skills in responding to the *PAS,* and those will be the subject of another book.

However, having said there is more information to come in other books in regards to adult and teen anger management, please understand that the general principles I talk about in this book not only apply to infants and children but also to everyone else. You can use the techniques I teach in this book on anyone.

Again, I hope you will get from this book what you are looking for.

Chapter Two: Conventional Temper Tantrum Wisdom

During all of the forty-plus years I have been parenting, the most consistent advice from tantrum "experts" has been for parents to ignore the tantrums. The theory behind the technique of ignoring tantrums, as I understand it, has been that ignoring tantrums prevents the validation of them. The ignoring parent avoids rewarding the child for the tantrum and avoids reinforcing the negative behavior with any kind of attention.

According to this don't-reinforce-negative-behavior theory, in this situation the underlying assumptions are that the child is throwing the tantrum for the purpose of getting undeserved attention (which is negative behavior), and if the parent avoids reinforcing this negative behavior, it should go away, stop, and cease to occur. Despite this theory behind the ignoring-tantrums technique, throughout modern history of parenting advice, most "experts" who've recommended using the technique haven't claimed that it will prevent tantrums or stop them in progress.

A few decades ago, "experts" still weren't putting the word "prevention" in the same sentence as the word "tantrum." Their advice was given only to help parents know the best way to manage and deal with the tantrums, pretty much the same as it is today. However, today's parenting "experts" now teach parents to prevent *some* of the temper tantrums by managing the child's temper tantrum triggers, such as frustration, tiredness, and hunger. In other words, these "experts" teach parents to prevent the frustration, tiredness, and hunger in their children. They really aren't teaching parents to prevent tantrums in the face of normal living, which occasionally includes frustration, tiredness, and hunger.

9

One current parenting advisor, for example, initially claims to help parents learn to eliminate temper tantrums. He later clarifies that by "eliminate" he means to stop fifty percent of them in progress and prevent fifty to ninety percent of them from happening at all. This can be done, he explains, by incorporating his communication techniques and being vigilant for temper tantrum triggers.

My method of temper tantrum elimination and prevention is *vastly* different from other methods. I teach parents how to respond to their infants and children in a way that makes it totally unnecessary to be vigilant and to have to watch for temper tantrum triggers. This is because the typical infant and childhood frustrations no longer trigger temper tantrums.

I teach parents how to totally, one hundred percent eliminate temper tantrums from their child's behavioral repertoire so that there are no longer any temper tantrums in progress to have to try to stop, manage, handle, or deal with. I also teach parents how to consistently respond to a newborn infant in a way that the child never develops a pattern of throwing temper tantrums. I teach parents these skills with as much clarity as possible and with many examples in the hopes that they will be able to learn them quickly and easily.

You might be wondering why I refer to other parenting advisors as "experts" (with quotation marks that suggest a negative attitude on my part). Also, given that I claim to know the secret to preventing and eliminating temper tantrums, you might be wondering why I don't refer to myself as an expert (without quotation marks). By using the quotation marks in referring to other professionals I mean no disrespect to those who actually have expertise. And I don't have a problem with assigning expert status to myself and others solely based on the word's meaning, which is as follows:

- **Noun**: A person who has a high level of skill or knowledge relating to a particular subject.
- **Adjective**: Possessing, involving, or showing great ability, dexterity, understanding, or knowledge based on experience and/or training.

I *do,* however, have a big problem with attributing expert status to parenting advisors who adamantly tell parents that temper tantrums are unpreventable and a normal part of all children's development (which is most parenting advisors, in my experience). My opinion (based mostly on my personal success with totally eliminating and preventing temper tantrums in my own children and others) is that these advisors are mistaken on this premise.

In fact, I believe the professional advice I heeded at the beginning of my parenting career—that tantrums are inevitable and should be ignored—contributed greatly to the temper tantrum behavior of my first five children.

I finally learned to stop blindly trusting "expert" status and I chose to be, as much as possible, an informed consumer of parenting and other advice. I learned to consciously assess the advice of professionals while putting it to a test, or to get second opinions before following advice that seemed questionable. I came to believe that this is *my* life, and it's up to me to minimize my wasted time and energy from following faulty advice.

An additional problem I have with assigning expert status to myself and others is the connotation that accompanies it: that the "expert" is the person in the advising relationship that is the healthy, functional, educated, or wise one and that the recipient of the advice is the unhealthy, dysfunctional, uneducated, or unwise one. I believe that using the term "expert" creates this unnecessary and disrespectful imbalance in the advising relationship. In my opinion, this alone is adequate reason to avoid the use of the word.

So, to recap, these are the reasons why I am using quotation marks with the word "expert:"

- As a challenge to the connotation that the advisors know it all, and the advisees know nothing.
- As a caution to advisees to critically evaluate all advice they are given (and to not blindly follow advice forever after just because of the professed "expert" status of the advisor).

Instead of "expert," I much prefer to call myself a mentor, which I define as:

- A wise and trusted advisor or teacher.

The term "mentor" has not acquired the same aforementioned connotation that "expert" has, plus "mentor" implies an earning of the trust involved, which is as it should be. I believe the "mentor" designation creates a more respectful dynamic in the advising or helping relationship. My methods of preventing and eliminating temper tantrums in children are based on the concept of respect, and hopefully so is my style of sharing what I've learned from my experience.

Let's get back to conventional temper tantrum wisdom. Have you ever witnessed (or been subject to) a tantrum in progress during which a parent (perhaps yourself) was actually following the traditional ignore-the-tantrum advice? Perhaps in a store, a child or infant was in a screaming rage. The parent responded by (1) ignoring the tantrum and the child, (2) remaining calm and cool, (3) acting non-chalant and unruffled, and (4) as quickly as possible (while maintaining an unhurried demeanor) getting through the checkout and out of the store. All this was much to everyone's relief, except probably the child's—whose anger by that time had escalated to an extreme level.

Let's look more closely at this paradigm. (I promise—that's the only super-annoying scholarly word I will use in this whole book.) Dealing with tantrums by ignoring them is part of a decades- or possibly centuries-old parenting model or set of assumptions, concepts, values, and practices that constitutes a misguided or wrongheaded way of viewing temper tantrum reality.

The "experts" have all along been telling parents to ignore tantrums simply because (according to them) it's unarguably the best way to deal with tantrum behavior in children. But "experts" mostly admit that responding by ignoring will not change or eliminate the tantrum behavior—because, after all, tantrum behavior in children is normal, natural, and inevitable.

MegaMom Tantrum Theory:

> **Tantrum Probability**: Tantrum behavior + responding by ignoring = tantrum behavior.

This circular theory begs a few questions. What measure is there for parents to employ so they can know if they're ignoring the tantrums well enough or thoroughly enough? *Just kidding.* I don't think anybody asks that question. But seriously, how can parents know if ignoring tantrums is even a valid and beneficial technique like the "experts" say it is?

There's absolutely no success or change to measure and nothing with which to evaluate this technique's effectiveness. In fact, it doesn't purport to be "effective" by way of creating a change. Using this technique is not supposed to solve anything. If the tantrum behavior stays the same or even gets worse, parents are just supposed to keep responding by ignoring simply because the "experts" say so.

And that's what I did at the beginning, as a novice parent. I consistently ignored the tantrums of my first four children until each of them outgrew the tantrum behavior, typically at about the age of two as the parenting advisors predicted they might. I also responded by ignoring the tantrums of my fifth child until I discovered that this technique was actually contributing to and provoking his tantrum behavior.

I learned that ignoring tantrum and pre-tantrum anger is part of the cause of tantrums. And I learned that as long as tantrums are ignored they continue to occur.

MegaMom Tantrum Theory:

> **Tantrum Probability**: Pre-tantrum anger +
> responding by ignoring = tantrum behavior.

After belatedly discovering this truth—that ignoring tantrums and pre-tantrum anger actually provokes tantrum behavior—and learning a few related tantrum truths, I developed, tested, and proved my new theories on my fifth child, and every additional child thereafter. Unfailingly, I was able to prevent tantrum behavior when I finally stopped ignoring the tantrums and started to respond to them in a functional way.

In total, I've succeeded in raising temper-tantrum-free children more times than I've failed, and all of my failures occurred before I discovered what I needed to change in my parenting style. Many people I've passed on my insights to (including some of my grown children) have reported back to me that my methods have also worked with their children.

I can and will (in detail and with confidence) tell you what causes, provokes, prevents, and eliminates temper tantrums in babies and children. And I can tell you that if and when you implement my methods (which I call Infant Anger Management), your child's tantrum behaviors are supposed to stop, go away, and disappear.

MegaMom Tantrum Theory:

Solution Probability: Pre-tantrum anger or tantrum behavior + Infant Anger Management = no tantrum behavior.

If you apply my Infant Anger Management techniques, and they ultimately don't work to totally eliminate or prevent temper tantrums in your child, I see only three feasible explanations for the lack of success. They are:

1. You aren't yet understanding or implementing my methods well enough.
2. You have a parenting partner or assistant caregiver who isn't using the techniques.
3. Your child has something else going on that a medical doctor or mental health professional should help you assess.

This is not to say that I view myself as perfect or all knowing in all things parental. But, based on my lengthy experience and assessments of these particular techniques (which I sincerely believe can succeed with all children in general), I believe that any lack of success with them in totally preventing and eliminating temper tantrums would not be the fault of the theories or techniques.

For parents who see some improvement but not total elimination of tantrums, I would suggest the first of the above lack-of-success explanations is most likely. For parents who see improvement for one caregiver and not another, the second of the explanations is most reasonable. And for parents who see no improvement whatsoever, I would highly suspect the third reason or possibly the first reason in the extreme.

Unlike traditional ignore-the-tantrum advice, Infant Anger Management techniques have a thirty-two-year track record of eliminating tantrum behavior and making a discernible difference. Ultimately, you should be able to judge the validity of these methods from your own experience.

Before I get into the nuts and bolts of my tantrum prevention methods, I do need to go over some theoretical concepts. Speaking of theory, I once was given the exciting gift of a gourmet sauce cook book. It turned out to have four chapters of sauce theory before getting into the alrighty-then-let's-make-sauces! part of the book. So much for gourmet sauces in *my* kitchen. I know theory can be boring and tedious, but I'll try to make it not.

So why has conventional temper tantrum advice, historically and currently, not helped parents rid the world of their children's temper tantrums? In addition to the faulty concept that ignoring tantrums is a beneficial technique, there are three misguided and wrongheaded concepts that conventional temper tantrum advice is based on.

Misguided Concept Number One:

Babies less than one year old (or for sure less than six months) are incapable of experiencing real anger and of throwing real temper tantrums.

16

Many child development theorists and a variety of related professionals have perceived newborn infants as not yet emotionally functional human beings—that is, not yet able to experience real live emotions. Many of the professionals I have researched have written that babies cannot feel real anger until six months to one year or more of age. Every angry-sounding expression of younger babies is not real anger, they say. Not that these are some *other* kind of anger or fake anger, false anger, pre-anger, or simulated anger, but not any kind of anger at all. Rather, we're told, they are simply instinctual crying responses to hunger and other discomforts.

It's unclear as to what these professionals believe happens at the magical age of six months or one year that enables babies to finally actually *be* angry when they *sound* angry. But I'm guessing that, in their minds, it's probably something akin to a baby gradually developing fine-motor skills or gradually gaining the ability for language.

Decades ago, when I was researching this particular child development theory and realized that I disagreed with it, I asked myself, "How did they come up with the perception that newborns are pre-functional in the emotional department?" It's not like we can see that the screaming infant is or isn't actually angry like we can see that a baby can or can't yet pick up tiny objects. By definition an emotion is a mental state that is un-seeable, and we can only interpret our perception of its expression.

Here's an example of what I mean. If spouses appear to be angry with each other, it is not a guarantee that they are. Conversely, if spouses appear *not* to be angry with each other, there is no guarantee that they aren't. It's quite easy to imagine adults experiencing different emotions than what they appear to be feeling. In reality, only the person with

17

the emotion can know, for sure, what is or isn't going on emotionally for them. Logically, that concept also applies to children and infants, and child development specialists have no actual ability to know that an angry-looking child is not really angry.

I don't know exactly how current theorists arrived at this scientifically unproven concept of infant emotional pre-functioning, but, in partially absolving them, I'm thinking they must have been taught this at university (including at the Masters and Doctorate level). That's where they studied the accumulated knowledge of the previous generation of child development theorists. That generation may have learned this belief from their behaviorism-based ancestral scholars, who generally viewed as irrelevant—even for adults—all subjective phenomena, such as emotions.

It appears to me that somebody, somewhere, sometime just made this concept up out of thin air and most of the other theorists went along with it.

In addition to this generational passing on of what I believe to be a mistaken child development theory, we've also had dysfunctional social theories and practices that contributed to the dehumanizing, devaluing, and emotional discounting of infants and children (among other social groups). As examples, children were the legal property of their fathers, they could legally be subjected to physical and emotional abuse by parents, and they were expected and taught to be seen and not heard.

It was common in my childhood days for crying children to be confronted with the parental warning, "Shut up, or I'll give you something to cry about." Thankfully, this kind of emotional neglect has greatly diminished in the childrearing of more recent decades. Despite the historical social failure to recognize infants and young children as fully functional emotional beings who have equal rights to feel and express their emotions as adults, our current knowledge can help parents to now recognize the very real anger and tantrums of their very young infants and children.

MegaMom Theory:

Newborns are real people with very real emotions. They can and do sometimes demonstrate real anger, even potentially from the minute they are born, and maybe even before. Assume, for a few moments, if you will, that newborns are certifiably fully functional emotional beings. And imagine that *you* are about to be born. You have not yet learned your language, but you can still see, think, feel physically and emotionally, and react to what goes on around you. You experience the following.

After a confusing, scary, squished, and pressured ride, you poke your head into the world and take your first surprising breath. Waaaaaaahhh! You squint against the annoying bright lights and whimper. You gag on the intrusive, sucking, poking thing in your throat and try to scream for help. Aaa...aaaa...ahhh! You are grabbed by a human shape and turned, and abruptly you start to slip and slide the rest of the way, right out of your private room. Whooooaaa! You try to hang on, but there's nothing to grab and your arms are pinned. You feel helpless. You pop into the cold, drafty, foreign, frightening place and shriek. Waaaaaaahhh!

You're lost and scared and you want to know just exactly what is going on, but you have no way to know. You startle with all the banging and clanging. Waaaaaaahhh! You have a very serious top-of-your-head ache. Waaaaaaahhh! You shiver as your wet skin starts to dry in the cold air. You hear happiness and you're offended that your misery is not being addressed. You want to go back to your warm room and make the scary, attacking shapes go away.

Panic-stricken and angry, you wonder where your warm water went. You squeal in your very best language imitation, "Give it back!" But they don't. They poke you. They prod you. They come at you with a sharp thing, and you yell the equivalent of, "Don't cut that. It's mine!" But they pay no attention. They cut off your lifeline, leaving you detached. They jostle you. With wetness still evaporating from your skin, they place you on your back on a wiggling, wobbling contraption, and you flail. Again, you scream your multitude of fears and angers at them. Waaaaaaahhh!

This is the *worst* day of your life! And *nobody* cares.

Of course, this exercise proves nothing. But it demonstrates some immediate situations in which newborns could potentially experience anger if they were capable of it. Thirty years' worth of observations of effective anger-calming methods has convinced me that newborns are indeed capable of feeling anger.

When infants' needs are unmet, anger is their natural human reaction. And in my parental experience infant anger can and does escalate. Furthermore, even newborn infants can actually interpret parental response (or lack of it) to their anger. By that I mean newborn infants (who desire the same kinds of responses to their anger as do older children and adults) are very aware of whether or not the responses they get meet their anger needs.

If infants consistently don't have their anger needs met, they learn to trust that likelihood, and they become predisposed to escalate quickly to temper tantrums. On the other hand, if infants consistently *do* have their anger needs met, they learn to trust *that* likelihood, and they become predisposed to *not* escalate to temper tantrums. In other words, the total prevention of temper tantrums in two-year olds can start as soon as they are born. This is done by teaching them that their anger is understood and will consistently be responded to appropriately. (I will be explaining later on what I mean by an appropriate anger response.)

Misguided Concept Number Two:

The causes of temper tantrums are the children's low tolerance for frustration, inability to express themselves with words, lack of problem solving skills, lack of other ways to let out their emotions, need for attention, and determination to get their own way, all of which naturally lead to tantrum experimentation.

MegaMom Theory:

**These things are not the real causes of tan-
trums. They are the causes of the initial anger
that precedes the tantrums. If a child's initial
anger invokes the needed response from a
parent, the anger will quickly go away and not
develop into a tantrum. One of the real causes
of temper tantrums is the parent not meeting
the initial anger needs of the child.** (Again, I
will be explaining what kind of responses children
need to their pre-tantrum and tantrum anger.)

Misguided Concept Number Three:

**Temper tantrums are a normal, natural, inevi-
table, and highly unpreventable part of raising children. Tantrum-free child rearing is not
possible, so we might as well hunker down
and tough it out until the tantrums naturally
disappear by the child's fourth or fifth year (at
the latest).**

It's not difficult to see where this misconception came
from. (Besides, that is, that it has been handed down for
generations.) I don't know for sure how many children each
parenting "expert" has had on the average, but, from my
admittedly limited pre-Internet, pre-Wikipedia library
research twenty years or so ago, it appeared to be maybe
one or two. And I seriously doubt that the average number
of children per "expert" has increased in the last two decades. I've noticed that disclosure of biases is not all that
common among book-writing "experts" and many of them
won't say how many children they've had. You often have to

guess their family size by how many people they've dedi-cated their books to. It's true.

Now, personally I did have a lot of parenting skills figured out at the very beginning of my parenting, as most parents do, but certainly not everything. Many things unexplainably took years for me to learn. Some things took a specific child to learn on. Some took specific circumstances to learn in. And some required prerequisite learning of other things. Perhaps some things took readiness or maturity on my part.

I don't believe any parent can possibly know all there is to know about parenting by one or two preschoolers or even by one or two teenagers. I learned some very crucial skills with my fourth and fifth children. I'm still learning things after forty-one years on the job. It's common, though, for parents to want to hide their parenting imperfections. No one likes to openly admit (especially with something as important as parenting) that they have faults or failings or even a lack of knowledge.

There are some people, though, who seem to actually and truly believe (and some who even declare) that they have achieved early-on perfection in their parenting abili-ties. Most of us have probably met at least a few of these boasters. I've noticed, though, that most of them typically start to come out of their delusional thinking patterns somewhere around the time their child enters elementary school and provides them with some publicly embarrassing, rude awakening sort of behavior. Truly hard core "perfect" parents, though, may not be provided with such helpful eye openers until their child's teen years, or on really rare occasions, never.

Anyway, here's how I think it works. Many parenting "experts" (who got that status mostly from attending college and not so much from raising children) obviously have an even deeper-than-average parental need to present as "perfect"—I mean over and above the normal it's-not-fun-to-admit-your-mistakes kind of thing. When they present themselves as "experts" in raising children, the accompanying implication is that they are "perfect" at it.

Soon after becoming parents the "experts" suddenly have temper-tantrum-throwing children of their own. This proves to them their textbook theories about the universality of tantrums because if even themselves, the "experts," raise tantrum throwers, certainly no "inexpert" or average parent could possibly do better. Right?

But—and this is a very big but—if ostensibly all children throw tantrums, then how do we account for parents of the self-confessed imperfect variety who insist that their child or children have never thrown a temper tantrum? I've met some of them, and I'll bet you have too. Are they simply all lying to us? Or is the theory of tantrum inevitability just plain wrong? I believe the latter.

Parents of tantrum-free children may not all know exactly everything they do that's different from what the parents of tantrum throwers do, probably mostly because they typically don't have "failures" to compare with their "successes" like I did. In other words, I'm guessing that most parents who raise tantrum-free children are able to do it with all of their children, right from the very beginning of their parenting. Somehow they get on the right track at the start and don't follow the prevailing tantrum advice. They don't usually do the before and after like I did, being able to articulate, "Here's what I did when I was failing, and here's what I changed in order to succeed."

But even if these parents can't tell us exactly how they raise tantrum-free children, they still provide evidence for my theory. They still demonstrate that tantrum-free child rearing is possible for those who somehow manage to figure out the right techniques.

MegaMom Theory:

Tantrum-free child rearing is possible and preferable. And compared to the alternative, it is a much more enjoyable form of parenting for everyone involved, including the general public.

Chapter Two Summary: Temper Tantrum Wisdom

- Parenting "experts" have consistently advised parents to ignore tantrums so as to not reinforce the child's negative behavior.

- Tantrum Probability: Tantrum behavior + responding by ignoring = tantrum behavior.

- Tantrum Probability: Pre-tantrum anger + responding by ignoring = tantrum behavior. (Ignoring a child's initial anger is part of the cause of tantrums.)

- When infants' needs are unmet, anger is their natural human reaction.

- If infants consistently don't have their anger needs met, they learn to trust that likelihood, and they become pre-disposed to escalate quickly to temper tantrums. On the other hand, if infants consistently *do* have their anger needs met, they learn to trust *that* likelihood, and they become predisposed to *not* escalate to temper tantrums. In other words, the total prevention of temper tantrums in two-year olds can start as soon as they are born. This is done by teaching them that their anger is understood and will consistently be responded to appropriately.

- The causes of temper tantrums are NOT the children's low tolerance for frustration, inability to express themselves with words, lack of problem solving skills, lack of other ways to let out their emotions, need for attention, and determination to get their own way. These things are the causes of the initial anger that precedes the tantrums.

- If a child's initial anger invokes the needed response from a parent, the anger will quickly go away and not develop into a tantrum. One of the real causes of temper tantrums is the parent not meeting the initial anger needs of the child.

- Tantrum-free child rearing is possible.

MegaMom's Wisdom for Tantrums

Chapter Three: Tantrum Epiphany; How I Discovered the Secret

So what was it that started me on the road to tantrum-free child rearing? Let me describe to you the epiphany, the milestone incident.

For some reason I can't remember, I was visiting in the home of a woman in my small town. She had some university education (I believe in something like psychology or social work). Somehow we got on the topic of temper tantrums, and she stated authoritatively something like, "Kids throw tantrums so we'll know they're angry." Now, some of you might think that concept would have to be obvious to any parent. However, until that moment, it hadn't been to me. But in an instant I recognized its truth and the very exciting possibilities it opened up to me.

Outwardly, I'm keeping my cool *[but inwardly it's a jumble of cartwheels and back flips and yahoos, and, "That's it! That's the clue I've been missing!" I'm trying to suppress my excitement and my inner emotional gymnastics while I assess rationally if that tidbit of wisdom (that I had unfathomably never been able to come up with myself) would help me eliminate my current baby's tantrums]* when this woman knocked me off the thought train I was excitedly on by telling me how she deals with her six-year-old son's tantrums.

["Wait a minute," I'm thinking. "You just knowingly shared the probable clue for the potential cure for temper tantrums, and now you're saying

29

that your six-year-old son throws tantrums of the kicking, screaming, writhing-on-the-floor variety? Unbelievable! My kids' tantrums only occurred until they were two or so, even though I was quite the tantrum-inept parent, in my own opinion. Okay," I'm thinking, "Something's wrong with this picture. Something's very wrong with this picture."]

[I'm still trying to find a way to mentally reconcile this conceptual discrepancy] when this kindly woman shared with me the words of her typical response to her son whenever he threw his floor-level tantrums. She apparently always said the same thing to him, *[which, I'm thinking, can not remotely communicate to him that she actually understands he is angry. And shouldn't that be the goal of parental communication if his tantrum is indeed for the purpose of letting her know he is angry, as she declared it is? Shouldn't her goal be to let him know that she knows he is angry?]*

However, this neighborly woman's stated response to her son was always something sarcastic and funny at his expense, such as: "Surely, honey you can do better than that. I don't believe the neighbors can hear you, sweetheart. Can't you scream louder?"

[At this point in the conversation I'm thinking, "No! Back up! You say he's throwing a tantrum so you'll know he's angry. Soooooooo… what if instead of being sarcastic to him—which probably makes him even more angry—you somehow effectively let him know that you understand he's angry? Shouldn't that terminate the tantrum? And then the next time, what if you let him know that you get that he's angry even before he makes it to the floor? Wouldn't that

30

eventually lick the problem altogether? Shouldn't that end his need to throw the tantrums?"]

[I'm totally convinced at this moment that I'm onto something BIG and MOMENTOUS, despite this woman's inexplicable misapplication of the common sense concept she has just taught me. At the same time, possibly out of embarrassment for my in-experience, I'm not at all letting on to her how excited I am about my new knowledge. I'm simultaneously conversing with her; assessing the new conflicting in-formation; pondering how to use it in my parenting; and concealing and channeling my too-intense inte-rior acrobatics into the more sustainable, yet still in-toxicating and thrilling, emotional activity equiva-lent of slow waltzing.]

I was only twenty-five years old at the time of this event. I hadn't yet found it important to even finish high school, and this other woman was a dec-ade or two my senior, who (for all I knew) might have had a couple of doctorates that I was more than capable of being intimidated by. So, I'm pretty sure I didn't in any way point out to her the contra-diction in her two-part friendly advice. I'm pretty sure I just politely laughed at her funny-from-a-parents'-perspective tantrum comeback while I felt some empathy for her son.

[Inwardly, though, I'm anxious to race home and finally start my Tango lessons!] I couldn't wait to experiment with and apply what I had just learned and to see what it could potentially do for my fourteen-month-old son. This was the first tan-trum information I had ever come across that sounded like it had some horse sense attached to it. And nothing else had worked, so far.

As it turned out, my interpretation of the wise tidbit this woman shared with me (which was that I needed to communicate to my baby that I understood when he was angry) ended up being only the first piece to the tantrum-be-gone puzzle. It turned out to be the pre-epiphany if you will.

In fairness to the friendly neighbor who gave me this first piece to the puzzle, I must explain what I have since learned about her sarcastic responses to her son. I initially thought they were a misapplication of her insight but later realized they likely weren't actually connected to her insightful understanding at all (and she had never claimed that they were). In recent years I read a decades-old parenting advice book that explicitly advises parents to do just what she had done—say something sarcastic to children during their tantrums. My guess is that my neighbor learned this particular tactic—one that I don't personally advocate—from that same parenting "expert."

But, despite my confusion over her tantrum responses, my neighbor's wisdom gave me a kick-start on the right track to ending and eliminating tantrums in my children. From applying my neighbor's wisdom—the first piece of the puzzle—I was able all on my own to come up with the second and even more important piece—the secret of Infant Anger Management. Before I share with you the actual changes I made in my parenting style with my fifth child, and then from birth on with my last eight children, however, I want to share my definition of temper tantrums and some general thoughts about anger. *I know—groan—more theory!*

MegaMom Definitions:

Temper tantrums come in two varieties: ***Type-One Tantrums*** and ***Type-Two Tantrums***.

Type-One Tantrums

A Type-One Tantrum is simply a true expression of anger that has escalated to rage—maybe to the extreme—and possibly to the maximum. A Type-One Tantrum is anger out of control or nearly so. It can look and sound many different ways. It may be solely expressed in a verbal way by screaming, crying, or raging. Or it may be accompanied by creative physical enhancements such as breath holding, body stiffening, kicking, flailing, or even attacking.

(Children are not the only tantrum throwers. Adults can and do throw them, too—both the Type-One and Type-Two versions. The physical enhancements of adult tantrums are often different from those of children, though. Whereas babies and children are more likely to engage in the above-mentioned types, adult tantrum throwers [especially not-quite-mature wives] are more likely to do such raging behaviors as smashing computers, ramming vehicles, or making bonfires out of spousal clothing.)

This Type-One Tantrum definition necessitates the inclusion of escalated newborn anger that occurs when the infant's needs are not met quickly enough. Technically this type of tantrum is preventable. But in reality, no parent (not even one who buys the best surveillance baby monitor or hires the best nanny) can always attend to the baby's needs before escalation occurs. Some babies scream for their food within a second or two of waking up. No parent could possibly rush out of the bathroom, hop out of the shower, or jump out of bed at night to have a bottle ready each and every time before the baby escalates. For this reason, each infant

33

will experience a few "starter tantrums" before learning to trust the empathy response to them.

This definition of Type-One Temper Tantrums does not include the screaming of an injured, pained, or very sick infant or child, even though some anger is usually present. In other words, this kind of raging, by its very nature, is almost totally unpreventable. It also usually starts out near the maximum level instead of escalating gradually.

Also, I don't consider this kind of screaming to be a tantrum because any anger involved is probably peripheral to fear and whatever instincts infants may act upon to ensure that parents are aware of their physical danger. Nonetheless, the raging of injured, pained, and sick infants and children is often easily diminished or stopped by using the same techniques that help eliminate and prevent actual tantrums. I promise I will share those techniques soon.

Type-Two Tantrums

A Type-Two Tantrum is a combination of an expression of anger (which could be genuine, unexaggerated, exaggerated, or even totally fake) and a conscious or deliberate element of manipulation or intimidation. This is the kind of tantrum that post-toddlers tend to throw (and in my case, my first two husbands). A Type-Two Tantrum may be precipitated when your child has been denied something, such as a new toy. She then, in conjunction with a show of real or faked anger, deliberately makes an attempt to manipulate, intimidate, or shame you into changing your mind.

This is the kind of temper tantrum that multitudes of parenting advisors caution you severely not to give in to because you would be reinforcing the negative and manipulative behavior of the child. I agree with the multitudes on this point. Don't give in. Respectfully stand your ground and don't let the tantrum thrower get away with the manipulation or intimidation.

To prevent and eliminate Type-Two Tantrums, you need additional skills (which I will also share with you) besides the ones you need to eliminate Type-One Tantrums.

Type-One Temper Tantrums, without breath holding and such, are generally not recognized in our society as tantrums (especially when they occur in pre-toddlers). As I've said, we've been taught by child development theorists that babies can't experience real anger, and many people still believe this. Also, we all know that it's natural for babies to cry by way of communicating, and this also helps camouflage baby anger.

Unfortunately, these concepts have helped many people believe that enforced crying is beneficial to babies. (I'm always amazed whenever I find this belief has filtered down into the practice of some of today's young parents. I somehow expect the current crop of parents to be more enlightened than those of past generations.) Anyway, as this absurd enforced-crying theory goes, crying helps develop baby lungs and stamina and prevents the "spoiling" of babies. By this theory's definition, a "spoiled" baby is one in need of an excess of attention or holding and is manipulative or demanding in order to get it.

My experience is that always doing the opposite of enforcing crying (that is, in meeting infants' needs as soon as possible) teaches them to trust, to be patient and content, to feel cared for and loved, and to not be at all demanding or manipulative. It teaches babies that parents consistently care about meeting their needs and that they don't have to demand what parents will quickly and willingly provide in response to their very minimal signals for help. Babies that typically get quick parental response to their needs get into a habit of giving minimal signals.

I believe enforcing crying does the exact opposite. It teaches babies that they have to cry or scream for what they need or want—sometimes for lengthy periods of time—and that sometimes they still won't get it. Enforced crying actually trains babies to be demanding, in my opinion. Also, I think it forces babies to feel regular anger towards parents, which could potentially harm post-babyhood relationships.

It's good to remember that infants do have legitimate needs to be cuddled, rocked, and held. (Just like we adults sometimes do—even if we can't admit it.) Therefore, we should try to recognize, validate, and meet infants' needs to be held. Personally, I'd rather give more holding than a baby asks for instead of less. Rocking a baby to sleep is a sweet, loving, caring, bonding experience. Letting a baby cry until asleep isn't. Oh—and about lungs—it's my experience that they tend to develop perfectly fine without enforced wailing. To my knowledge, I never produced a lung-deficient child.

None of my children ever threw Type-Two Tantrums. Not to say they never manipulated or intimidated—they just didn't do it in tantrum format. My first five children all threw Type-One Tantrums, with enhancements, probably all starting at around six to ten months old. I'll give you a couple of descriptive scenarios.

One time, I was at a social event when I abruptly left my fourth baby on the lap of another woman while I left for a few minutes to deal with some minor crisis. My son was familiar with this woman and he never made strange with anyone, so I didn't even suspect he would throw a tantrum in response to my leaving. But when I got back a few minutes later, he'd almost passed out from holding his breath, had thrown himself backwards, and had badly unnerved the woman who was carefully holding him.

36

Whenever something happened to make my fifth baby angry, he would scream and hold his breath, sometimes to the point of going limp. He would often stiffen his body and throw himself backwards from a sitting position, one time splitting open the skin on the back of his head on the track of the patio doors before I could reach him.

These two scenarios are typical examples of the super-fast escalation of anger into Type-One Tantrums that was a pattern with my first five babies.

In the next chapter, I'd like to share my perspectives on anger.

Chapter Three Summary: The Epiphany

- There are two varieties of temper tantrums: *Type One* and *Type Two*.

- A *Type-One Tantrum* is simply a true expression of anger that has escalated to rage—maybe to the extreme—and possibly to the maximum. A Type-One Tantrum is anger out of control or nearly so. It can look and sound many different ways. It may be solely expressed in a verbal way by screaming, crying, or raging. Or it may be accompanied by creative physical enhancements such as breath holding, body stiffening, kicking, flailing, or even attacking.

  o Type-One Temper Tantrums, without breath holding and such, are generally not recognized in our society as tantrums (especially when they occur in pre-toddlers).

- A *Type-Two Tantrum* is a combination of an expression of anger (which could be genuine, unexaggerated, exaggerated, or even totally fake) and a conscious or deliberate element of manipulation or intimidation. This is the kind of tantrum that post-toddlers tend to throw. A Type-Two Tantrum may be precipitated when your child has been denied something, such as a new toy. She then deliberately makes an attempt to manipulate, intimidate, or shame you into changing your mind.

  o This is the kind of temper tantrum that parenting advisors everywhere caution you severely not to give in to because you would be reinforcing the negative behavior. I agree. Don't give in to the manipulation!

Chapter Four: Anger

Anger is an emotion that functions as a signal to its owner and other involved parties that something is wrong, out of whack, or out of balance. We've all felt that signal with our own anger, but we don't always take advantage of it by using it to figure out what we need to fix in our lives and how to go about it. Examples of situations that will provoke the anger signal are when we perceive that our needs or wants aren't being met, we're in pain, someone's taking advantage of us, someone puts us in danger, too much is being expected of us, something isn't fair, someone violates our rights, someone abuses us, or someone doesn't care enough about us. It's natural and functional to feel anger in those kinds of circumstances.

Anger is meant to alert us, protect us, and get us to deal with such issues. Sometimes (you may have discovered this) when we do actually deal with an anger-producing issue, we discover that it was only or partially our perceptions that were out of whack, and the situation was not at all what we thought it was. (For example: I'm thinking the people at my bank messed up on my account. I go in to get them to clear up their mistake, only to find out that *I* was the one who messed up.) At such times we're really glad that we used respectful anger expression skills (if we did) or we're highly embarrassed (if we didn't).

Depression is an example of what can happen when the anger signal (or the warning) is repeatedly disregarded. People often feel angry about something but can't deal with the anger or the situation. They then suppress, ignore, or retreat from the anger and the situation through some level of "shutting down" or "tuning out" from the world. Often when depression sufferers go back to look at, acknowledge, and deal with their suppressed angers, they automatically start to come out of the depression.

So if you ever feel depressed, you might want to get out a pen and paper and write down any and all things you are angry about and then try to think of what you might do to fix the problems. If you find there is suppressed anger underneath a depression, you might be able to get rid of the depression simply by acknowledging the anger and trying to solve the problems that caused it. That is, if you can somehow get yourself to pick up the pen in the first place.

One really important thing to remember about anger is that it isn't good or bad in and of itself. As I've said, it's simply one of the emotions humans experience to help them recognize problems that need to be fixed. But people often don't get this about anger because of how they've been taught to perceive it and deal with it (or not).

You've probably heard the saying about money: that the love of it is the root of all evil. Or in other words, some things that are done out of greed for money are evil, or some things that are done *with* money are evil. But many people interpret the saying to mean that money *itself* is evil. It's the same with anger. Many people have been conditioned to believe that anger itself is bad, in addition to the harmful things that can be done *with* or *in* anger.

Some of the harmful and abusive things people can do with their anger are name-calling, blaming, verbally or physically attacking, controlling, abandoning, or intimidating others. In responding to other people's anger, we really need to not confuse their emotions of anger with their expressions of anger. We need to allow the emotions and not try to shut them down or put a lid on them, and we need to functionally respond to people's either appropriate or inappropriate expressions of anger. Of course, if someone is violent in their expression of anger towards us, either emotionally or physically, we need to protect ourselves from their violence.

A lot of people fear anger and conflict. Fear of someone's violent or abusive expression of anger, of course, is a very legitimate fear. But fear of the emotion of anger is kind of like the fear of mice—not considering Hantavirus—it's not very valid. Think about it. Someone's emotion of anger isn't going to hurt you. And you won't be hurt by a mouse running under your chair, by a nest of baby mice falling on your foot on the gas pedal as you drive—as I once had in farm country, or by a mouse running between you and your underwear while you contort out of your clothes—as my former father-in-law once had, also in farm country.

Really, have you ever been hurt by a mouse? I think probably not. You likely have only ever been startled by one. Likewise, anger itself isn't going to hurt you (though it may startle). So if we haven't already, we need to get over our fear of anger. We need to learn to tolerate it and develop non-abusive, non-embarrassing anger expression skills. Anger (like mice and such) is part of the human condition, and we need to practice good healthy ways of expressing it and responding to it.

Let me give you just one example of an anger expression skill—using "I" statements instead of "You" statements. Making a "You" statement (especially when angry) tends to come across as accusatory, blaming, and implying intent. This usually invokes a defensive response, which isn't likely the purpose of expressing the anger. "I" statements don't do those things.

Let me demonstrate the contrast between the two. Here's a "You" statement: "You didn't pick up your toys as soon as I told you to, and now there isn't time." The implicit messages in this statement are: "You made me angry, you are at fault, you meant to upset me, and you'd better not do it again." In reaction to "You" statements, most people will defend themselves instead of apologizing.

Conversely, an "I" statement could be: "I needed you to pick up your toys right when I told you to, and now there isn't time." Even if these words were said in an angry tone, the implicit messages are: "I'm angry that your toys aren't picked up. I wish I had followed up earlier. And I needed your help." "I" statements tend to help the speaker take appropriate responsibility in situations, or at least it sounds more like the speaker is taking responsibility even if not conscious of doing so.

My guess is that a large majority of people in our society are not yet in the habit of using "I" statements instead of "You" statements in times of conflict and anger. Most of us have had the disadvantage of not learning this skill in childhood. I can attest, however, that it is entirely possible to develop this skill in adulthood to a point that it becomes automatic—where you don't even have to think about it for the most part. All it takes, really, is consciously and consistently trying to use "I" statements in times of conflict. The results are so worth the effort that it quickly becomes easy to remember. And eventually it becomes automatic.

The reality is that lots of people don't have good anger expression skills. Many people have learned to avoid conflict by suppressing their own anger and ignoring or shutting down the anger of others around them. Lots of people can't even admit when they're angry (especially if they're newlyweds). And tons of people don't have the ability to discuss their anger or the issue they are angry about in a rational way with the person they are angry with. Most people don't get this kind of training in their upbringing or anywhere else.

As a society, we've learned to view anger itself as bad. (Especially when it comes from females, who are always supposed to be sweet, nice, kind, cheerful, positive, long-suffering, patient, supportive—all of that—but never angry.) You've likely heard the long-standing admonition to moms; that they are responsible for setting the proper emotional "tone" in the home, which proper "tone" almost guarantees there won't be any discord between family members. What horse pucky!

Every person in a home should be equally allowed to experience their own emotions and, according to their age and ability, should be accountable for contributing to the positive emotional atmosphere in the home. What mom can't testify to having set the proper tone and then had dad or one of the kids come along and unset it? Oh yeah, it's every-body's job! That's my opinion.

But anger itself is not bad. Anger is just an emotional signal—like other emotions are signals. Fear signals us to take protective action. Embarrassment signals us to behave more appropriately or maybe stay away from certain people. Sadness signals us to properly grieve for our losses (and maybe learn from our choices) so that we can move on in a healthy way. And anger signals us to figure out what seems unfair towards us and whether or not there is anything non-abusive we can do to fix it. (And fear of mice signals a hasty trip to the hardware store.)

Chapter Four Summary: Anger

- Anger is an emotion that functions as a signal to its owner and other involved parties that something is wrong, out of whack, or out of balance. Anger is meant to alert us, protect us, and get us to deal with perceived personal violations. Anger isn't good or bad in and of itself.

- In responding to other people's anger, we really need to not confuse their emotions of anger with their expressions of anger. We need to allow the emotions and not try to shut them down or put a lid on them, and we need to functionally respond to people's either appropriate or inappropriate expressions of anger. Of course, if someone is violent in their expression of anger towards us, either emotionally or physically, we need to protect ourselves from their violence.

- A lot of people fear anger and conflict. Anger (like mice and such) is part of the human condition, and we need to practice good, healthy ways of expressing it and responding to it.

- The reality is that lots of people don't have good anger expression skills. Many people have learned to avoid conflict by suppressing their own anger and ignoring or shutting down the anger of others around them. Lots of people can't even admit when they're angry.

- Anger is a legitimate emotion that functions as a warning for us to deal with perceived personal violations. And temper tantrums are nothing more than escalated anger (either real or faked) with or without an element of manipulation.

Chapter Five: The Secret

Okay, back to my story.

Fresh with my new insight—kids throw tantrums so you'll know they're mad—I reasoned that if this was true, then my babies had not known that I actually *did* know when they were angry. They had probably been desperately trying to clue me in all this time, getting more and more frustrated and angry in the process. All while I diligently ignored their tantrum behaviors. They must have wondered, "Is she stupid, or does she just not care?"

The escalation of my children's anger from the beginning point to the tantrum stage was usually very quick. Nonetheless, I reasoned that if I was somehow able, in a way they could understand, to acknowledge the anger before it got to the tantrum stage, I most likely could prevent the escalation of their anger. So the very next time my fourteen-month-old son started to become angry, I quickly, verbally acknowledged his anger. I gave it a name. (I used the word "mad" because I thought it easier for a young child to learn than the word "angry.")

This naming and acknowledging of an infant's or child's anger is an important beginning part of the process in dealing with temper tantrums. (Many parenting advisors, in fact, do tell parents to name the emotion to the child.) However, despite my initial high hopes of this being *the tantrum key*, I found that it actually wasn't the most crucial part of preventing or eliminating tantrums.

The real secret to dealing with, eliminating, and preventing temper tantrums is something that I learned immediately after I consciously acknowledged my son's anger that first time.

Whatever it was that had caused his anger, it probably was something I had failed to do for him as quickly as he

45

wanted it done because when I told him that I understood he was angry, I also apologized to him. I can't remember what I apologized for, but, in an **empathetic** tone of voice I told him I was sorry. He settled down immediately instead of escalating like he normally would have done.

Somehow I knew that his positive reaction of calming down much more quickly than usual was much more likely due to the empathy I had just given him than to my acknowledgment of his anger. At that moment common sense kicked in, the mega light bulb went on, the super lightning bolt struck, and the primary epiphany occurred for me.

I pondered: He calmed down *so* well when I empathetically apologized for my lack of speed in meeting his need. I wonder if he would do the same thing if I weren't slow in meeting his need, but I still gave him empathy for his experience of anger and for whatever he went through that led to his anger. **In other words, was it basically empathy that would always end my son's expression of anger?**

I tested out this new empathy concept and found it to be the consistent antidote to tantrums. From then on, whenever my son showed any anger, I did all of the following:

- Immediately stopped what I was doing.
- Quickly found out what was going on for him.
- Tried to understand what he was angry about.
- Told him empathetically that I was sorry he was mad, and I was sorry he'd had to go through whatever it was that had sparked his anger.
- Hugged and physically comforted him in an empathetic way.
- Directly apologized in an empathetic tone of voice if I had inadvertently or accidentally failed to meet his

needs quickly enough or committed any other offenses that I could discover.

I empathized *nonstop* each time he was angry until he was no longer showing signs of anger. It worked beautifully every time! It only took a week or so and just a few angry episodes before he stopped his tantrum behaviors entirely. His expressions of anger became much quieter and much shorter. Thus they became extremely easy to empathize away.

It was obvious to me at that point that empathy was always the primary thing my son wanted when he was angry. I came to know that **giving empathy in response to children's anger is the secret, the key, the trick, and the answer to curing, eliminating, stopping, preventing, and dealing with their anger and their temper tantrums.**

I want to pause here and make sure we're all on the same page when I'm talking about giving **empathy**.

MegaMom Definition:

Giving empathy is communicating in a verbal and/or physical way with other people that you understand their situations and motives and that you care about their feelings and difficulties.

Feeling empathy and giving it does not require an alignment with the recipient regarding thinking, values, or beliefs. In other words, you don't have to agree with people, believe they made good choices, feel the same way they do, or even like them to feel and give them empathy. To *feel* empathy for them, you only have to understand, identify with, and care

47

about their misery and suffering. And *giving* them empathy only requires that you somehow communicate that genuine understanding and caring.

MegaMom Theory:

Infant Anger Management:

Tantrum behavior + empathy response = instant lessening of tantrum behavior.
Tantrum behavior + consistent empathy responses = total elimination of tantrums
Pre-tantrum anger + consistent empathy responses = total prevention of tantrums.

I call this system **Infant Anger Management** (which suggests that it only works with infants) when, in reality, if you can apply it properly, it works for people of all ages. In just three words my title implies the following important, however not yet widely accepted concepts:

- Infants can and do experience anger.
- Infant anger can be effectively managed.
- Tantrums can be totally eliminated if infant anger is consistently and effectively managed some time after the onset of tantrums.
- Tantrums can be totally prevented if infant anger is effectively managed from birth on.

I believe this title has the potential to help dispel the myth of the universality of preschooler tantrums and to bring attention to the very real possibilities for tantrum social reform. But I don't believe there is any danger that the use of the Infant Anger Management system will be limited to infants, despite the title. Anyone who uses it with infant or toddler tantrums will likely know enough to use it with the anger of their older children, spouses, extended family, neighbors, coworkers, customers, and even strangers. Anyone who uses it successfully on infants and small children will likely be able to see the value in applying it universally.

Let's get back to my story for a moment. It was obvious to me that my 14-month-old baby understood the empathy I was finally giving him. He was obviously intelligent and mature enough to know what was going on in my before and after responses (ignoring vs. giving empathy). He must have thought, "Holy cow! She gets it! She cares! About flippin' time! Yeeesss!" He almost instantly learned to trust that I understood, cared, and would be empathetic whenever he was angry.

If empathy were not the secret to preventing tantrums, or if my baby were incapable of understanding my expression of empathy, he would not have become permanently temper tantrum free within a week or so of my new application of empathy. He would have continued his more than half-a-year habit of throwing tantrums, just like all of my previous children had until about the age of two.

Giving empathy for anger (no matter the age of the angry person) is not an automatic and typical thing to do in our society. Most of us certainly did not *receive* empathy for our own childhood anger. Angry children in the fifties and sixties, for example, were much more likely to get a smack than empathy. Actually, I think I was probably in my late twenties or early thirties before I ever *heard* of empathy, let alone received any.

People who view anger as bad or who experience fear or discomfort in the face of anger or conflict aren't likely to automatically *feel* empathy for an angry person. They are more likely to feel uncomfortable or fearful and try to avoid or *shut down* the other person's anger. This social reality may be a big part of the reason why other parenting advisors have not come up with the real temper tantrum antidote all these years; many of them may have been uncomfortable in dealing with anger, also preferring to avoid it or ignore it.

Despite the general discomfort that many people experience when dealing with other people's anger, responding to child or adult anger with empathy is a very simple, relatively easy thing to do. It's not so easy when the anger is expressed in a scary or abusive way, but even then it's *possible* for the experienced empathy practitioner (though it may not always be safe). With babies, it's *way* easy because it's pretty hard for a functional person to be intimidated by or judgmental of a baby's anger. Giving empathy is so simple. In fact, it's such a simple cure for temper tantrums that you may doubt my assertions that it can totally, universally work.

Just in case you are a doubter, I want you to consider a scenario that may help you more on an emotional level to understand that it works. Here it is.

I want you to pause and picture yourself angry. Really angry! Imagine that on your way to work you got a $300 traffic ticket for making a left turn on a yellow light. And you had already entered the intersection *before* the light turned yellow! I know! Outrageous! Three hundred dollars for turning left on a yellow light—not a red light! Ludicrous!

Now I personally know this couldn't possibly have happened in Utah where I currently live. In Utah you can, while fiercely applying your useless brakes, glide through an icy intersection seven seconds after the light turns red, blaring your horn and steering in-between two vehicles (luckily missing them both) and not even get a traffic ticket from the kindhearted officer who closely observes your red-light violation from the opposite direction.

So, definitely, the yellow-light, left-turn ticket could *not* have happened in Utah, but it did happen to one of my adult children. I'm not making it up. A word of caution—if you're going to drive through Lethbridge, Alberta, Canada, you might want to avoid left turns as much as possible. Just in case.

Okay, back to your anger scenario. So you drove through Lethbridge on your way to work and you are mad! (You're also late at this point.) How would you feel if you told your coworkers what happened, and every one of them absolutely ignored you as if they hadn't even heard what you said? Would you feel like looking for a new job, perhaps? How would you feel if someone said matter-of-factly, "I can see that you're angry."? You'd probably wait for further comment, thinking, "Aaaaannnndddd?" What if someone only said, "Bummer!"? You might think: "That's it? One word? On an anger scale of one to ten I'm probably up to a six here, and you can only muster one measly empathetic word?"

Seriously, what anyone would naturally want from a group of coworkers in such a circumstance would be a healthy helping of empathy, including some or all of the following: "How awful! That's *so* unfair! There's no law against that! What was that officer thinking? You need to report him. Three hundred bucks? That's an outrage! You should be able to fight that in court, but then you'd have to take time off work. What a bummer! I'm so sorry this happened to you. I'll be impressed if you're able to get *any* work at all done this morning. Can I get

51

you something? You can have my cheesecake—you need it a whole lot more than I do. Do you want a hug?"

Most people would also call home or call a friend on their coffee break, hoping to get more of the same. And many people would repeatedly tell the story to every neighbor and acquaintance they happen upon over the next day or two (and even total strangers at the convenience store and such), hoping to glean a little more empathy.

What you and I really want and need when we're angry, more than anything else, is for someone to give us a healthy dose of empathy for our situation. My experience is that infants and children want and need the same thing. Preventing the escalation of their anger is mostly about the empathy response.

Now, it may be so obvious that I shouldn't need to even mention it, but—just so it's clear—if an infant's or child's initial anger is due to unmet needs (such as hunger), a caring and empathetic response *has* to include the meeting of the need. (That is, feed the baby ASAP).

MegaMom Theory:

The cause of Type-One Temper Tantrums (or non-manipulative anger escalation) is the lack of a timely, caring, and empathetic response from the parent to the initial anger. It may also involve a too-harsh or not-loving-enough tone of voice (which I will discuss soon).

Let's get back to my chronicle. My fifth child had become tantrum free. Thereafter, right from the birth of each new child I had, I applied these same techniques whenever they showed anger. That is, I acknowledged the anger and gave adequate amounts of empathy *while* giving as much physical comfort—such as hugging and rocking—as possible and appropriate.

The younger the baby, the more exaggerated was my empathetic tone of voice. A typical scenario might be that for a few minutes I didn't hear my newborn crying because I was at the other end of the house. She's now angry about me not arriving fast enough with her food. My empathy response might include the following words:

> Oh, baby, I'm so sorry I didn't hear you. Poor baby. You're so mad. Poor baby. Okay, I'm getting your bottle as fast as I can, honey. Poor baby, you're so mad. I'm so sorry. Okay, your bottle's almost ready. Just one more minute. Here it comes. Poor baby. There you are, sweetheart. Poor baby.

Some of you might be wondering how the anger of newborns can be alleviated by empathic words when young infants can not possibly understand the meaning of the words. The reality is that they don't need to understand the words because they somehow understand the tone of voice used in the delivery of the words. You could test this out by giving empathy in gibberish. It would work just as well— well, at least for a few months or so. Done longer than that, the infant might end up highly confused or might seriously question your mental state or your emotional reaction to anger.

Also, you might be wondering how I knew it wasn't the bottle, instead of the empathy, that provided the relief from the anger. I knew because the baby's anger started disappearing as soon as I gave the comforting and empathy, prior to the bottle arriving. As well, I'd been giving bottles without empathy for years. Certainly bottles could and did end the anger without empathy, but they didn't do it nearly as quickly as they did it with empathy. The addition of empathy always speedily reduced anger levels and, overall, increased infant patience and tolerance.

Another thing you could be wondering is whether or not I gave empathy in the typical high-pitched voice that it's so easy to slip into using when speaking to babies and children. *Absolutely not!* Personally, as an adult, I've always found this high-pitched manner of speaking to babies and children *so* annoying to listen to. I think I would definitely feel patronized if someone spoke to me like that.

I believe babies and young children probably feel the same way as I do about this—although they can't possibly articulate it and maybe can't even conceptualize it. But if babies can get empathy from a tone of voice, surely they can get *condescension*. I imagine a baby thinking: "Uh, Mom, I really wish you wouldn't talk to me like I'm stupid or something. I'm an intelligent human being ... just ... little."

I also didn't use baby talk or toddler talk with my little ones. I never made it a habit to speak to my babies or little children in deliberately short phrases, short words, or using much more facial expression or body language than I used with older people. Of course, I did those things sometimes in play, but that's not the same thing as deliberately using these techniques with the idea that young children can not otherwise understand adults. (As I said previously, I did use the word "mad" instead of the word "angry" because I thought it easier for my babies to learn, but that was because they were only newborns when I started using it.)

Successful communication with babies and toddlers is more in the tone of voice than anything else. As I said before—the younger the angry baby or child—the more dramatic emphasis I put into the expression of empathy. This was not about acting goofy, silly, or childish in an embarrassing way, but rather it was about speaking more emphatically than usual in an effort to get the baby's attention and convey sincerity.

In order to get cooperation from my toddlers and totally avoid their temper tantrums (including in public), I have not had to embarrass myself by talking and behaving like a toddler as some other professionals recommend. I have found it crucial, however, to sound firm and loving when trying to get cooperation. And it's absolutely necessary to sound genuinely empathetic when the child is angry.

I'll give you an example of an empathy response given to an angry three-year old who had been conditioned since birth to expect empathy when angry. The child in this scenario is crying angrily and makes his way to me. Here is the conversation:

> "You sound mad, Tyler. Are you mad? What happened sweetie?"
> "Kevin took my truck!" By now we're on the floor, and Tyler is getting hugged on my lap.
> "Oh, I'm sorry. That's not fun, is it?"
> "Nope!"
> "Boy, sometimes it's *really* tough having a big brother, isn't it?"
> "Yeah!" Tyler's face breaks into a huge smile, and he stays cuddled on my lap until he has absorbed enough empathy and is ready to go do something else, or until he decides to go have a chat with Kevin.

So the empathy responses on my part taught my last eight children early on (and the first five not so early on) that they could trust me to understand, care, and consistently nurture them when they were angry. It also taught them (both female and male) that anger is an acceptable emotion to express.

All of this promoted self-nurturing, which is a very good thing for children to learn. I'm serious. Any one who doesn't learn to self-nurture early in life runs the risk of developing the potentially traumatic inability to re-connect with their imaginary "inner child"—should they ever attempt "inner-child" work in adult group-therapy sessions. It's true. A good, healthy, self-nurturing habit throughout childhood can spare adults the anguish of this kind of pop-psychology treatment embarrassment. And who knows, maybe it can even spare them the treatment itself.

My last eight babies each did, of course, experience *some* escalated anger a few times. This was typically when I didn't hear them cry right away as tiny newborn infants...well the nine- and almost eleven-pounders weren't so tiny. These episodes were simply normal bouts of newborn hunger crying that lasted a couple of minutes—nothing more. It only took these few essential trust-building "starter tantrums" to teach my babies that I would be consistently empathetic whenever I didn't meet their needs fast enough. Conversely, all of the times I did meet their needs quickly were simultaneously teaching them to trust me in that area.

These few initial "starter tantrums" were always swiftly and easily calmed by my empathy responses. The amazing thing is that the combination of generally meeting a newborn's needs quickly and giving empathy in a few less-than-quick situations causes the newborn to no longer experience escalated anger when a need isn't met quickly. Very young babies are conditioned by these methods to be relatively patient, trusting, and anger free. (Of course, every baby has patience limits.) But compared to my first five children, the last eight were much more contented as babies. They cried very little and were very patient. They were much less likely and much slower to escalate in their anger.

Here's another difference between mine and typical tantrum advice. As long as I've been paying attention, parenting advisors have been telling parents, "Don't try to reason with a child during a temper tantrum." They often state that children less than the age of two are generally too young to reason—period. Personally, I don't think any of us are able to reason particularly well in the midst of a rage. But if I'm raging, and someone starts feeding me empathy and mixes in a little reason—honestly—I'm not going to stop ingesting the empathy to pick out the chunks of reason. I'm going to consume both.

And I might actually get a taste of the reason before I swallow it. But for sure, *once* it's swallowed, I'm going to digest it and be nourished by it. And the more empathy I've swallowed, the higher the concentration of reason I will be able to handle and pay attention to. Little kids are capable of the same functioning, in my experience. However, dishing out reason *without* empathy to a child during a tantrum definitely doesn't help. That's obviously a recipe for escalation disaster, for sure.

Let me give you an example of what I'm talking about here. Let's say eighteen-month-old Jimmy starts screaming because Billy grabbed a toy away from him and bopped him on the head with it. Billy then ran to the bedroom with the toy, slamming the door shut. Here is a sample mixture of empathy and reason (with the reasoning words written in italics). Words like these might be given to Jimmy, all in a very empathetic voice:

"I'm so sorry Billy took your toy and hit you. [picking Jimmy up] Let me see your owie. Poor sweetie! [Hugs and kisses] *It should feel better in a couple of minutes.* But it really hurts right now, doesn't it? That sure wasn't nice of Billy. You're really mad at him, aren't you? I'm sorry you're mad. It's not fun being mad, is it? I'll bet you want him to say sorry to you. *And I'll bet he wants you to say*

57

sorry for pushing him over when you were watching cartoons. Maybe he's still mad, too. You guys sure aren't having a very good day, are you? I'm sorry Billy hurt you and took your toy."

This example does not address the conversation that is also needed with Billy. He probably could use some parental empathy as well, some helpful advice as to how to best interact with Jimmy, and a clear message that hitting is not allowed. I would recommend the confiscation of the disputed toy until both parties are willing to reconcile.

Here are my further ideas on babies and reasoning:

Number One: No one really knows just how soon after birth humans can actually reason. I think it's probably younger than generally believed by child development theorists. I have seen and heard numerous things over the years that have contributed to this thinking.

My earliest-to-talk child, at barely six months old started communicating somewhat unusually. She had heard me walking down the hall and wanted to tell me that her older sister was changing her diaper. As I came in sight, her face and shoulders were turned towards me. She raised her voice quite loud and excitedly said her first word, "dipa!" From that point on she regularly communicated with words that matched her circumstances, which indicated not only her understanding of the words she was using, but her understanding of the circumstances as well.

In my previous experience, babies of that age and even up to ten-months old only really did word and sound repetitions and weren't able to demonstrate their understanding of many words and situations, beyond recognizing their own name and other simple commands. I'm not saying I think they didn't understand words and situations—just that they weren't able to verbally demonstrate their understanding. My point is that we might be typically giving babies far too little credit when it comes to their reasoning abilities.

Even more amazing than my daughter's early verbal skills were those of one of my grandsons. I was so astounded by his utterances that I kept track of the dates of some of them. Although he couldn't yet articulate all of the English language sounds, this grandson first began speaking in sentences (mostly with correct pronouns) starting at the age of six and a half months. He pleadingly said, "*I hungy!*" to his mom who was walking by with some pasta. A few minutes later he pled, "Hungy!" to his dad who was walking by with an ice cream cone. This grandson sporadically spoke in sentences from that day on.

Before this child was eight months old, when his Mom was putting him to sleep against his wishes, he said, "I wan' my Amma!" He meant he wanted me, Grandma. At ten months old he started regularly saying, "I wuv you!" to both of his parents. Also at ten months old he loudly and insistently repeated his best rendition of his own name until I recognized what he was saying.

At twelve months old, whenever anyone was upset or crying, this little baby would caringly ask them, "You okay?" At that same age, my husband jokingly blamed something on him when a bunch of us were visiting around my dining room table. He was just a little baby bouncing on his dad's lap, turned away from us. He stopped his bouncing, turned to look my husband straight in the eye, and said, "It wasn't me."

At a year-and-a-half old, every week from the grocery cart, this grandson would demand, "Gamma fowers! Gamma fowers!" until his mom chose a bouquet for him to give to me. (He'd been in my flower garden many times the previous summer, and I had recently given him a book that pictured a child in his grandmother's flower garden.)

Also at a year-and-a-half old, there was one person in this grandson's life who regularly talked to him in a high-pitched voice and one who was not respectful in other ways. Every time this little boy shut the front door after one of these people left, he would announce to the room, "He's *soooooo* annoying!"

I still don't know how such effective verbalizations are even possible at such a young age, except that it might have something to do with an unusual ability to memorize. This child's mother could mimic every TV commercial at the age of two. At five years old (so I've been told) on weekdays she memorized the entire scripts of two soap operas (that I swear I don't remember ever letting her or any other child watch). She then reenacted both of these soap operas for her older sister after school. Also, since her preteen years, she's been able to perform, with voices and songs, the entire script of any Disney movie you choose to be entertained by.

It couldn't have been just a memory thing with this grandson, though. Despite having a mother with photographic and phonographic memory capabilities (that she unfortunately did not even remotely get from me), he wasn't just memorizing and repeating words he'd heard. His sentences always matched the situations, and he always spoke with appropriate and adult-like emotional emphasis. It always felt like listening to and interacting with a child at least three or four years older than he was.

This child was also very observant as a baby. He learned on his own, much earlier than typical, how to do such things as turning the computer on and off and opening and shutting the garage door for people.

For many years I've thought that very young children are capable of a lot more thinking and reasoning than what is commonly believed. My little prematurely verbal grandson, who is now almost seven years old, only strengthened those beliefs. I don't think he was particularly more capable of thinking and reasoning than most children, just that he had exceptionally early verbal skills that let us see the cognitive level he was at.

Number Two: Communications with children that are based on underestimations of their abilities to reason are a form of "talking down" to them. I believe children generally understand when we're underestimating them and are offended by it. Conversely, communications with children that are based on an overestimation of their reasoning capacities could, at best, help them feel respected and included. At worst, they could cause the children to think, "Huh? What? I didn't get that."

Number Three: When helping infants deal with their anger, it's pretty easy to run out of empathy words and phrases. As I said before, what can it hurt to throw in some reasoning ones in an empathetic tone of voice? Who knows, the baby might listen and actually understand or maybe be further distracted from the anger by trying to figure out what the adult is talking about. My experience is that it does no harm to try to reason with a very young angry child if the reasoning is well mixed with empathy.

One very empathy-laden reasoning tool that works well with angry people of all ages is to tell them empathetically that you wish you could give them what they want, but you can't. Then explain why. I found as an airline baggage-service agent that I could regularly turn irate in-my-face adult travelers into acquiescent patrons with the words: "I wish I could give you a new piece of luggage, but the airline rules state that the damage has to be all the way through to the inside of the main part of the bag. I'm sorry, but I can't cover this damage to your bag."

A young child that is used to receiving empathy can often be placated with statements like the following: "I wish I could let you eat more candy right now. But I can't because I have to protect you from making yourself sick like you did last Halloween. I'm sorry, but I'm going to have to make you wait until after dinner. Would you like a carrot stick while you wait?"

Sometime after I proved to myself the overall effectiveness of my tantrum prevention techniques, I devised an infant *Empathy-Awareness Test.* My main motive for doing this initially was to further prove my relatively new theories. But I also used the test with each new baby I had in order to confirm and demonstrate to myself each particular baby's empathy awareness. And I used it to demonstrate to my teenagers still living at home, who babysat for other people and who might someday become parents, that young infants can and do understand when they are receiving empathy.

I also taught my *Infant Anger Management* method in general to all of my teens living at home, but they didn't always use the method when they tended my younger children. I remember one toddler reacting with near-tantrum-like behavior to an older sibling who didn't give her empathy when she was angry. But this toddler never threw tantrums with me—because I consistently had given her empathy since birth.

Here's how my *Empathy-Awareness Test* worked. When a baby was maybe three or four months old, I would watch and wait for an episode of anger. When it happened I would comfort, empathize, and soothe the baby (as usual) into a quiet state. This was often done in a rocking chair.

After a minute or two, while still holding or rocking the quiet, contented infant, I would give *more* verbal empathy (exactly like what had just soothed the baby). Without fail, the baby would first start to whimper and then start crying angrily again (only to be quickly re-settled by continued empathy). It appeared to me that starting the second wave of empathy always had the ability to reconnect the baby's thinking with the upsetting event and the baby's emotions back to anger and self-empathy.

My *Empathy-Awareness Test* always convinced me that my very young babies could understand what empathy was all about. It also showed me that they were highly capable of self-empathizing and self-nurturing. This is a very important coping skill to learn in life because more often than not your own self is the only empathy-dispensing, nurturing individual available to you.

Chapter Five Summary: The Secret

- The real secret to dealing with, eliminating, and preventing temper tantrums is giving empathy *nonstop* each time the child is angry until there are no longer any signs of anger. Empathy is always the primary thing people need when angry.

- Feeling empathy and giving it does not require an alignment with the recipient regarding thinking, values, or beliefs. In other words, you don't have to agree with people, believe they made good choices, feel the same way they do, or even like them to feel and give them empathy. To *feel* empathy for them, you only have to understand, identify with, and care about their misery and suffering. And *giving* them empathy only requires that you somehow communicate that genuine understanding and caring.

- o **Infant Anger Management:**
  - Tantrum behavior + empathy response
    = instant lessening of tantrum behavior.
  - Tantrum behavior + consistent empathy response
    = total elimination of tantrums
  - Pre-tantrum anger + consistent empathy response
    = total prevention of tantrums.

- Despite the general discomfort that many people experience when dealing with other people's anger, responding to child or adult anger with empathy is a very simple and relatively easy thing to do. It's not so easy when the anger is expressed in a scary or abusive way, but even then it's *possible* for the experienced empathy practitioner (though it may not always be safe). With babies it's *way* easy because it's pretty hard for a functional person to be intimidated by or judgmental of a baby's anger. Giving empathy is such a simple cure for temper tantrums.

- The cause of Type-One Temper Tantrums (or non-manipulative anger escalation) is the lack of a timely, caring, and empathetic response from the parent to the initial anger. It may also involve a too-harsh or not-loving-enough tone of voice.

MegaMom's Wisdom for Tantrums

Chapter Six: The Second Part of Prevention and Elimination—Being In Charge (Part One)

I've given you the core concept involved in preventing and eliminating both Type-One and Type-Two Temper Tantrums—that of giving adequate acceptance, understanding, and **empathy**. But that's, of course, not all there is to it. Here is the second part.

MegaMom Theory:

The cause of *Type-Two Temper Tantrums* is a combination of the lack of a timely, caring, and empathetic response from the parent to the child's initial anger and also some form of the parent not being respectfully, adequately, or consistently *In Charge* of the child.

This concept of being In Charge is two-sided. The first aspect of a parent being In Charge of a child is for it to be done respectfully. The parent needs to be In Charge of the child in a firm, loving, fair, and non-harsh way. If a parent is disrespectfully In Charge of a child, the child may react with stubborn, manipulative, or retaliatory expressions of anger. In other words, a parent who is In Charge of a child in a disrespectful way can easily provoke temper tantrums in the child.

The second part of a parent being In Charge is about being In Charge enough (adequately)—and enough of the time (consistently). It's about the parent not allowing the child to be In Charge. If a parent consistently fails to be adequately In Charge of a child, the child tends to learn to

67

throw Type-Two Tantrums in a manipulative, disrespectful, continuous effort to stay In Charge of the parent and get what the child wants. I believe that repeatedly or consistently allowing a child to be In Charge (or simply lacking the skills with which to stop a child from being In Charge) is what causes Type-Two Tantrums to become habitual or ingrained.

My observations over the past few decades have been that not only do many contemporary parents of young children not seem to know *how* to be In Charge of their children, but more and more parents seem to not know that they even *should* be In Charge of their kids. I would love to see this trend start to reverse. I think parents and kids are suffering because of it.

Probably the most common type of comment other parents have made to me when they've found out how many kids I've had is, "How could you possibly handle that many kids? I can't handle my one!"...or "My two are more than enough for me!"...or, "My three drive me nuts!" I've been in this situation literally hundreds of times.

Sometimes in these circumstances I was able to see the parent's one child acting up as we conversed and I thought, "Your one kid would drive me nuts, too!" but of course I didn't say that. I also didn't say that the biggest likely cause for the huge difference in our parenting experience was the difference in who was In Charge of whom (parent In Charge versus child In Charge). What I did say was that parenting is a very difficult job. And it is.

I prefer to use the term "In Charge" instead of "In Control" due to the negative connotations associated with the latter. By being In Charge, I mean being the one or ones who are responsible, running the show, taking charge, in command, directing, managing, and in authority. By In Charge I don't mean "making every decision." Children need to be allowed and expected to regularly make decisions appropriate for their age. This concept of being In Charge is somewhat complicated. But it's not really difficult to master for parents who are convinced of its validity and its benefits. It's definitely worth the effort.

I will thoroughly go over, in this and the next chapter, all aspects of being In Charge. In this chapter I mostly share my analysis of my personal struggles with the concept and my related views on physical discipline, including how they evolved. I will also discuss at length the concept of power struggles and how they relate to the In Charge concept.

I openly admit that I've erred somewhat on both sides of this concept of being adequately and consistently In Charge in a loving, firm, respectful way. During the first seven years of my parenting career, I often didn't sound loving enough and I sounded a little too harsh while being In Charge. That contributed to my children's anger levels, to some power struggles, and I believe to their temper tantrums.

Also, when my first children became teenagers (but were all well past any danger of throwing Type-Two Tantrums), I had some difficulty standing up to their intimidation and disrespect and with remaining In Charge adequately and consistently enough. This was in addition to the typical everyday parental difficulty of remaining In Charge with teenagers. Later on I will share with you how I ineffectually tried to get back In Charge in that circumstance.

Let me tell you first how I discovered that I sounded too harsh and not loving enough. My fourth child as a toddler was a climber and thrower extraordinaire. As soon as he could walk, he inspired our use of paper plates by systematically unsetting the dinner table every meal until every plate in the house had ended in pieces on the floor. He regularly walked through relatively neat rooms leaving behind him thirty or more things on the floor in as many seconds. He was often rescued from the top of our seven-foot bookcase.

We had to keep the bathroom door shut at all times because for many months this toddler dipped cups into whatever liquid he could find and left them everywhere. His crawling baby brother simultaneously went through a stage of drinking every liquid thing he could find. Eventually, though, this little toddler mimicked our behavior, yelling "Uuuuh-Ooooh" whenever someone accidentally left the bathroom door open, slamming it shut to keep himself out. He would also run to us with items he wasn't supposed to be touching while he repeatedly yelled, "Uuuuh-Ooooh!"

During this period of time I was constantly exhausted from (1) keeping up to this toddler's nonstop adventures, and (2) having severe sleep deprivation and constant colds and flus because my fifth baby had extreme colic and woke me up ten to twelve times every night for his entire first year. Throughout this difficult phase, I often exchanged parenting stories with my friends, telling of my toddler's outrageous, often funny, and sometimes very challenging escapades.

While sometimes recounting his capers within his earshot, I started referring to him, somewhat affectionately, as "Dennis the Menace." I did this for a number of months until another mother challenged me by asking, "Don't you think he can understand what you're saying and that you might be perpetuating and encouraging his behavior by talking about it like this?" I had to agree with her. He could. And I might be.

Of course, analytical as I am, I then had to see if eliminating my "menace" talk—both the oh-isn't-that-cute kind, and the he's-*such*-a-challenge kind—would decrease his "menace" behavior. My little "Dennis" remained a throwing, climbing adventurer, of course, but he was much less intense and irritating after I stopped referring to him as a "menace" and talking about his behavior as I had been. I wasn't sure, however, just how much of his behavior improvement could be attributed to the elimination of my "menace" talk and how much was from my elimination of another thing.

In paying close attention to the things I was saying to and around my children (so as to self-censure the "menace" talk) and in observing their reactions, I just happened to notice other verbal behavior that I needed to improve. I detected that I had been sounding too harsh and not loving enough with my children. I could see the angry, defiant, and uncooperative responses I was provoking in them, including my pre-toddler.

Because I'm admitting my mistakes to you here, I feel entitled to explain how I think I fell into making them. I had been raised in a family almost totally free of physical discipline, and I started my parenting career declaring that I would never spank my children. This was more than four decades ago. Back then my no-spank perspective was quite unpopular and was generally perceived as parentally foolish and weak. Using physical discipline was the generally accepted norm.

My husband at the time seemed to have a mortal fear of raising spoiled children—for which he surely would have been teased by his extended family. (Their favorite pastime at get-togethers back then seemed to be to mock every absent family member, especially in-laws. Hopefully it's not like that any more.) Anyway, my husband repeatedly tried to pressure me into adopting his pro-spank point of view. His mother also tried to influence me. She told me that raising children was easy—all a parent needed was a big switch (preferably willow).

For the most part, in raising my children I did adhere to my strong belief that non-physical discipline was highly preferable to the physical. I made every effort to learn all the functional non-physical discipline methods I could from other people and parenting advisors, and I was always open to discovering some of my own. However, during my initial years of parenting while I resisted my husband's pressure to have me use the Spanking Method, I think I was somewhat influenced by his fear of being mocked by relatives for having spoiled children.

I believe I subconsciously compensated for not spanking in those early years of parenting by developing a communication style that was a little too harsh and not loving enough. I perceived spanking as physically harsh and perhaps I unknowingly opted for slight verbal harshness as the lesser but necessary evil. Nonetheless, however it had evolved, I belatedly recognized the pattern of my harsh tone during my eliminate-the-menace-talk research.

Upon this discovery, I decided immediately that I needed to modify and improve my tone of voice when dealing with my children. I decided that I should fix my tone of voice by sounding equally firm and loving. I didn't get this concept from any parenting book. I got it from overdue common sense.

I was able to fairly quickly convert to this kinder, more respectful, but still firm way of talking to my children. This almost instantly caused them to convert to a very cooperative and compliant way of responding to me. From then on, by consistently using a firm and loving tone of voice with my children, I was able to get overall, general compliance from every toddler and young child I had (except my ADHD, oppositional defiant disordered child).

I was embarrassed that it had taken me five children to learn how to get overall, general compliance from them, but I was also very excited. Having abandoned the too-harsh and not-loving-enough tone of voice I had been using, I was certain that I was no longer inciting temper tantrums and power struggles (more on those later) or provoking anger and defiance in my children.

I learned to use the firm and loving tone of voice with my children about half a year before I incorporated the empathy response to child anger into my parenting reper-toire. By itself, the firm and loving tone of voice did not stop my baby at the time from throwing temper tantrums, al-though, as I said, I believe it likely reduced the number of them. If I hadn't already converted to the firm and loving tone of voice, though, implementing the empathy behavior without it would have been problematic. The following generic scenario demonstrates what I mean:

- The parent sounds too harsh or not loving enough when dealing with the child.
- The child then feels disrespected and gets angry.
- The parent notices the anger and gives empathy for the situation that led to the anger—oops, the parent probably *cannot* give empathy for what really led to the anger be-cause the parent is unaware of the tone-of-voice failings.
- The parent either names and blames something else for the cause of the child's anger or leaves it unnamed.
- The child knows perfectly well what caused the anger and gets even more angry that the parent is so in denial, so uncaring, or so out of touch with the reality of the con-tributing behavior.
- The child then rejects the misplaced or unplaced empa-thy.

Learning both techniques (using a firm and loving tone of voice and giving empathy responses) was very important. It was very helpful and fortuitous that I learned them in the order I did. I might not have recognized the *secret* so easily, or it might not have appeared as such a consistent solution otherwise.

The following is a continuation of my overall perspectives on the physical discipline of children and it includes the exceptions I've made to my life-long no-physical-discipline rule.

I never did learn to prefer giving physical discipline to the non-physical. But when I was dealing with my first three teenagers and two preteens (plus three younger children), I halfheartedly tested out the Spanking Method in response to strong urging and scorn from my mother-in-law. I was only willing to try the method because my first few sons, who had absorbed some misogynistic attitudes from a close role model, were behaving quite disrespectfully towards me and I hadn't otherwise been able to resolve the issue. (My sons' disrespect included fairly regularly mouthing off to me and a rebellious household chore slowdown agenda over many months.)

This weeks-long physical discipline trial episode failed to get me back In Charge of my children. I just couldn't do it properly. My kids consistently laughed at my spanking efforts because (they said) I didn't hit hard enough for it to hurt. When I then forced myself to try the willow branch, the kids made a big joke of padding their pants, but still laughed at my inability to be harsh enough. I didn't have it in me.

In retrospect, I also concluded that these children had at the time been much too old to spank (another contrast to the standard pro-spank view). I eventually did, through learning to come up with and issue appropriate non-physical consequences, get the months-long rebellious situation reasonably under control and get back In Charge of my children.

Proponents of the Spanking Method could argue that it didn't work for me because I didn't give it a good enough try and I didn't cause enough physical discomfort to my children. I'm sure that's what my former mother-in-law would have said, had I consulted her. I would disagree.

During my spanking trial period, I mentioned to my husband that the method was not working and he chose to intervene a time or two by spanking the children hard enough to cause them some pain. (After that I was careful to revert back to my usual child-protection and annoyance-prevention practice of keeping him as much out of the child-rearing process as possible.)

What I observed when my husband spanked the children hard enough to cause them some pain was that it appeared to also cause them to feel some serious (and in my opinion justified) anger towards him. Even more disturbing was that it caused what appeared to be hatred from them towards him.

To supporters of the Spanking Method, I would admit that the technique, when done hard enough to cause some pain, may seem to succeed in gaining compliance from children. The method may cause children to comply because of their fear of further pain, their fear of what the parent might do next, or their fear of the parent. But at what expense is such compliance gained?

Might the child's fear or hatred of the parent result in ongoing or even deferred disrespectful behavior towards the parent? Might the child try to get even somehow with the parent for the disrespectful parent-to-child physical violence? My personal belief is that, in general, the negatives of using the Spanking Method in the traditional way far outweigh any positives that can come from it.

Eight years or so after my faulty trial of the Spanking Method, I was pseudo-single-parenting my fifth through seventh teens along with seven younger kids. By that time I had discovered a minor, non-abusive—in my opinion—physical method that I thought *did* work well in dealing with older children who "lipped off" or showed verbal disrespect to me. I found that a physical tap to the child (that wasn't hard enough to cause physical pain) worked as a message to the child that I would not tolerate such disrespect. Whenever I tapped a child in such a circumstance she always looked slightly embarrassed and did not continue "lipping off". And the tap did not cause any noticeable anger or resentment on the part of the child.

Prior to learning the Tap Method, a few times I had tried smacking a cheek for the "lipping off" offense, but I found cheek smacks provoked strong and lasting anger and resentment, so I discontinued them. Another traditional discipline technique that I early on found distasteful (pun intended) was to wash a cursing child's mouth out with soap. Once was enough for that resentment-producing method.

A physical discipline technique that I did feel comfortable using throughout my parenting was to physically move a location- or movement-resistant, defiant child, say from one room to another, whenever necessary. Small children I would simply pick up and carry. I preferred to move larger children by taking them firmly by the upper arm and pushing or pulling them as carefully as their level of resistance allowed me to.

I know some parents choose to move defiant children by leading them by their ears, but that seemed to me more likely to cause physical pain, which wasn't the point, so I didn't use that method. And I've seen parents move kids by their hair, but that method seemed outright abusive to me. Nevertheless, I felt, and still feel that most children occasionally act defiant enough to require an enforced physical relocation by the parent.

76

Late in my parenting career I found spanking to be the only discipline method that worked to get cooperation from one of my children who was ADHD and extremely oppositional defiant almost since birth. (Thankfully, I only had to spank her a little harder than I was comfortable with.) By the time this daughter was six years old, I had told her numerous times that she was much too old to spank and that she really should choose to be compliant—short of me spanking her. Unfortunately for both of us she did not make that choice.

All along I also kept trying every reasonable non-physical motivator with this child that there was—plus an unreasonable one that a counselor suggested (which had a fairly risky outcome and was also unsuccessful like all of the others I tried). I have since read of psychology research that claims a majority of parents who deal with severely oppositional defiant children actually give up on them and just let the children be In Charge.

I admit that I often felt like giving up on this daughter. But despite the horrendous difficulty of persevering, I couldn't give up. It just wasn't in me. I had to do my best to protect her from her own unwise choices. I kept trying to get through to her. She did eventually, gradually start to come out of her oppositional defiance mode when she was seventeen, after receiving some legal motivation.

Except for one other highly successful minimal physical discipline technique (that I will explain in the next chapter) this has been a complete accounting of what physical discipline methods I have tried and used with my children.

The rest of the chapter focuses on power struggles and what they are, what they look and sound like, how they work, what is really going on, what to do with them, what not to do with them, how to avoid them, how and when to extricate yourself from them, etc.

MegaMom Definition:

Power Struggle: A power struggle between parent and child, by my definition, is when parental authority is temporarily suspended during a non-physical battle between the parent and child over which one is In Charge. I'll give you a couple of examples. A simple version would be:

"I need you to pick up your toys right now."
"No."
"Pick up your toys, please."
"No."
"Pick up your toys!"
"No!"
"PICK UP YOUR TOYS!"
"NO!"

A little more complicated version would be:

"Dinner's ready."
"Meatloaf! I hate meatloaf!"
"Too bad."
"I'm not going to eat it."
"Yes, you are."
"No, I'm not."
"You only have to eat one slice."
"Uuh uuh."
"Eat it."
"Nope."
"You'll eat it if I have to spoon feed you."
"I won't."
"You'll sit there until you eat it!"
"I'm not eating it!"

"EAT!"

Power struggles are categorically un-winnable for parents. The reason for this is that during the power struggle parental authority is in suspension and the child knows it. By very definition, the parent has lost by giving up being In Charge and allowing the struggle. That alone guarantees that a power struggle taken to its conclusion is not going to be won by the parent.

Power struggles, I believe, are a very special and fun form of entertainment for kids. But kids are smart enough to not ever let on to this—it's a pretty well-kept secret. I believe also that power struggles are a means that children use—if they can be successful at getting them going—to push for more control over their own lives and diminish the control their parents have over them while they mature. Power struggles are intended to discombobulate parents.

Though no other factor is needed, another one that exists in the children-will-always-win-power-struggles dynamic is that children have unlimited amounts of time and energy to spend in thinking up and executing ways to perpetuate the struggles. In a lightning flash, any power struggle has the potential to become the top ongoing priority of a child, ahead of other beloved activities or even activity addictions (such as video games).

Conversely, parents have limited time and energy with which to engage in exhausting, lengthy, and emotionally draining power struggles. Parents find power struggles to be emotionally draining because even if they're not aware of it they've temporarily lost something crucial—being In Charge. Children don't have the same emotional reaction to power struggles because they haven't lost anything, plus they've gained an entertaining opportunity to interact with a disconcerted parent.

Parents who get embroiled in power struggles with their children—often because they don't have the skills to avoid them in the first place—often give up the battles in a sense of defeat or sometimes become angrily abusive in getting back In Charge. When parents do become abusive in getting back In Charge, they can easily make the tactical mistake of thinking they have won the power struggles. Children in such cases are just letting it appear that the parents have won because it has temporarily become too risky to continue.

What really is happening in these situations is that parents are operating training camps for hidden aggression. In other words, given enough occasions, these children learn to aggressively—using some unattributable or hidden means—get even with the parents for abusively appearing to win the power struggles.

Let me reiterate—children have unlimited time to think up a multitude of ways to get even with parents for abusively "winning" power struggles. I don't mean get even as in, "Okay, Mom gave me six ounces of trouble, so I'm going to give her *back* six ounces of trouble." Oh no—get even as in: "I'm going to give her back ten *pounds* of trouble. And I'm going to enlist every sibling, neighbor, and cousin I can find. This is going to be such fun!" *That's* the kind of getting even I'm talking about—the kind that can drag on for however long it takes the child to feel avenged.

Children, by their very don't-have-to-make-sense nature, are all potential masters at hidden aggression. By this I mean that what they do to get even with a parent for "winning" a power struggle requires absolutely no logical connection with any part of the topic of the struggle, the struggle itself, or even the general concept of the struggle.

The parent could try to uncover a suspected connection to an earlier power struggle in the motivation of any discovered, befuddling behavior of the child by asking, "Why did you do that?"

The child could simply thwart detection by declaring, "I don't know." (Of course, the child knows perfectly well that the parental force-feeding of the despised carrots was how come his dad's shoes ended up making polish marks across the master bedroom carpet.)

If the parent actually figured out the hidden aggression aspect of the child's behavior—which is highly unlikely because of the life-needs-to-make-sense nature of adults—and asked the child directly, "Did you put shoe polish on my rug because you were still mad at me for force-feeding you yesterday?" the child would simply deny it and profess ignorance of his own motives. Most self-respecting parents, however, would never ask such questions. Even if they were able to suspect such illogical connections, questions like these would unnecessarily put potentially new tactical ideas into their children's heads.

So, if not by winning or losing them, how *should* parents deal with power struggles? First of all, we shouldn't *provoke* them by sounding less than loving or by being too harsh or disrespectful to the child. Second, we also shouldn't *allow* power struggles by abdicating our parental authority.

When we tell a child to pick up the toys and he refuses, we should not restate the order. This would be the turning point. Restating the order to pick up the toys would be the parental action that makes it an official battle of ostensibly equal wills (which is an abdication of parental authority). Restating the order to pick up the toys would be the parental action that turns the conversation into an official power struggle. *We should not restate the directive for the child to pick up the toys.* Instead, at such times we need to maintain our parental authority and deal quickly and respectfully with the defiance of the child.

One method of dealing with such defiance with a very young child might be to take him kindly by the hand and get him started on picking up the toys, reiterating firmly and lovingly that this is when the toys must be picked up. For a grade- or middle-school-aged child it would be appropriate to respond to the refusal with, "You have two minutes to have it done."

If either child were to respond with further resistance, the parent could go straight to the Counting Method (which I will explain soon). If that technique fails to gain compliance—which isn't likely—then a consequence should be matter-of-factly issued. It's not necessary to always have a consequence figured out before notifying a child that there will be one. It's okay to say, "I will be giving you a consequence as soon as I can think of one that you won't like."

Power struggles over food (which are just as parentally un-winnable as any other kind) should also be defused before they ignite. Power struggles about food can provoke hidden aggression retaliation that may include the development of lifelong eating disorders. Instead of setting up a battle with the child, we should be respectful and offer reasonable choices. For example: "You can eat this now or eat something else when we have our next meal. Hopefully that will be more to your liking." It's even reasonable to declare what will be served for the next meal, if known.

One of my children, at the age of three, was an extremely finicky eater. I was finding it impossible to get him to eat numerous foods that he didn't like. Upon consultation, my family physician assured me I could solve the problem in a matter of days by giving my young son the above-mentioned choice with each meal he was resistant to.

An important part of the process was to not allow my son to eat anything between meals (which, of course, is much easier to do with a three-year old than with a more fridge-friendly preteen or teen). I was also assured by this doctor that no lasting harm would come to my son if he chose to miss an occasional meal or even to stubbornly not eat for a day or so.

It didn't take very long or very many missed meals (if any) until my little boy ate everything he was served, without complaint. However, I could always tell by the unpleasant expression on his face as he compelled himself to eat, which foods he didn't like.

Notwithstanding my good advice about avoiding power struggles, if you happen to discover yourself in the middle of one with your child, I recommend that you (1) stop; (2) take a deep breath; (3) remind yourself that you have *zero* chance of truly winning; (4) say something amicable like, "Whoa, how did that happen? We need to start over;" (5) start over where you should have initially disengaged from the battle bait; and (6) this time actually disengage, maintaining your parental authority. In other words, abandon the power struggle in progress and start over.

Whenever children suck us into arguments, they've trapped us in a sneaky version of a power struggle. Once I finally caught on to that, I declared a standard rule in my home that children were not allowed to argue with me. They *were* allowed to respectfully debate about issues, but they were not allowed to argue. They did anyway, of course. The rule was not so much intended to totally prevent all of their attempts to argue with me. It was more to allow me to easily extricate myself from any argument pits I accidentally slipped into.

One extrication technique I've used many times is to interrupt the argument in progress with the words, "Cease and desist!" repeated cheerfully as many times as necessary to shut down the argument. This process of repeating a verbal message numerous times is called the "broken re-cord" technique. Whenever I did catch on at the first hint of an argument, I could shut it down immediately by saying any of the following kinds of things:

- "Oh—what I just said—that was not an invitation for you to argue with me."
- "My decision is not negotiable."
- "I will not be swayed by harassment; I will only be an-noyed by it."
- "You can discuss the issue with me, but you are not allowed to argue it. If you don't know the difference be-tween arguing and discussing, I strongly suggest you forego this discussion at least until you've had the chance to figure it out."

    I don't advocate using the extrication technique of re-peatedly saying, "I love you too much to argue with you" like at least one other parenting advisor recommends. My main reason for not using this technique is that this vague decla-ration doesn't make sense. I don't refuse to argue with children because I love them too much. I refuse to argue with children because *I* am supposed to be the one In Charge and letting them argue with me is tantamount to giving up my position of being In Charge. That's the real and exact reason why I shouldn't argue with my children.

    If I were to offer to my child a no-arguments-allowed reason such as this one that doesn't make any sense, I would be encouraging my child to think I was lacking in intelligence. This is not something I ever want to do acci-dentally, let alone intentionally. Also, I think using the broken-record statement, "I love you too much to argue with you" would probably feel patronizing, disrespectful, some-what sarcastic, annoying, and perhaps confusing to chil-dren. I much prefer using a straightforward, honest, and easily understood approach to disallowing children's arguments.

The final objection I have to the I-love-you-too-much message about arguing is that it really only states that the parent refuses to argue with the child. It does not state that it is disrespectful or unacceptable for the child to argue with the parent. So the I-love-you-too-much message, in my opinion, is also a fairly weak message from an In Charge standpoint.

Chapter Six Summary: The Second Part of Prevention and Elimination—Being In Charge (Part One)

- The cause of Type-Two Temper Tantrums is a combination of the lack of a timely, caring, and empathetic response from the parent to the child's initial anger and some form of the parent not being respectfully, adequately, or consistently In Charge of the child.

- This concept of being In Charge is two-sided. The first aspect of a parent being In Charge of a child is for it to be done respectfully. The parent needs to be In Charge of the child in a firm, loving, fair, and non-harsh way. If a parent is disrespectfully In Charge of a child, the child may react with stubborn, manipulative, or retaliatory expressions of anger. In other words, a parent who is In Charge of a child in a disrespectful way can easily provoke temper tantrums in the child.

- The second part of a parent being In Charge is about being In Charge enough (adequately)—and enough of the time (consistently). It's about the parent not allowing the child to be In Charge. If a parent consistently fails to be adequately In Charge of a child, the child tends to learn to throw Type-Two Tantrums in a manipulative, disrespectful, continuous effort to stay In Charge of the parent and get what the child wants.

- I believe that repeatedly or consistently allowing a child to be In Charge (or simply lacking the skills with which to stop a child from being In Charge) is what causes Type-Two Tantrums to become habitual or ingrained.

- By being In Charge, I mean being the one or ones who are responsible, running the show, taking charge, in command, directing, managing, and in authority. By In Charge I don't mean "making every decision." Children need to be allowed and expected to regularly make decisions appropriate for their age

- **Power Struggle:** A power struggle between parent and child, by my definition, is when parental authority is temporarily suspended during a non-physical battle between the parent and child over which one is In Charge.

- So, if not by winning or losing them, how *should* parents deal with power struggles? First of all, we shouldn't *provoke* them by sounding less than loving or by being too harsh or disrespectful to the child. Second, we also shouldn't *allow* power struggles by abdicating our parental authority.

- *When we tell a child to pick up the toys and he refuses, we should not restate the order.* This would be the turning point. Restating the order to pick up the toys would be the parental action that makes it an official battle of ostensibly equal wills (which is an abdication of parental authority). Restating the order to pick up the toys would be the parental action that turns the conversation into an official power struggle. *We should not restate the directive for the child to pick up the toys.* Instead, at such times we need to maintain our parental authority and deal quickly and respectfully with the defiance of the child.

MegaMom's Wisdom for Tantrums

Chapter Seven: The Second Part of Prevention and Elimination—Being In Charge (Part Two)

In order to prevent Type-Two Tantrums, it is super important that parents be In Charge of their children and not vice versa. However, Type-Two early childhood Tantrums, even with multiple years of violent and manipulative kicking and screaming bouts, are *nothing* compared to the potential horrors when a Type-Two Tantrum thrower matures into an In Charge teenager or an In Charge adult child in the home.

I swear, in general I'm not a fear monger, but if anything ever should dictate a little instilling of fear in the hearts of parents, it's the concept of teen or adult children being In Charge of the parents. Very serious and possibly even life-threatening parenting troubles can result from grown children being consistently In Charge. Troubles such as intimidation or abuse from children, financial ruin, adult-child occupation of the parental home, pre-inheritance or pre-senility asset takeover, or even (worst-case scenario) a premature pulling of the parental plug: "*Sigh*. Comas are so boring, Mom. You've had a whole two hours. Time to go. Bye."

Because being In Charge is so important in child rearing, I'm going to discuss at length ways to accomplish it. But, first, here are a few foundation thoughts:

MegaMom Theory:

1. Children are dependent human beings who are in the process of learning to be independent adults In Charge of themselves. Sometime in mid-childhood,

89

or possibly much earlier, it is usual for children's desire for independent experience to regularly exceed their readiness for it.

2. Parents are entrusted to monitor and safely direct the maturation process of their children. Some parents, often starting when their children first achieve mobility, develop an overactive protective impulse to curtail independent childhood experience. All parents must constantly make independent-experience decisions for their children—decisions for which they will certainly be judged both too lenient and too strict by various outside observers (and when involving preteens and teens, for which they will certainly be challenged).

3. Children push for perceived overdue experience that might, in actuality, be premature. Parents have a responsibility to limit their children's experience to what they believe the children can safely handle, but the limitations they establish might, in application, be overprotective. This dynamic sets up the inevitable and constant vying to be In Charge between parents and children. The very existence of this dynamic necessitates the development of some basic parental survival skills, those being: how to *be, remain*, and regularly *get back* In Charge. I will discuss those skills periodically throughout the rest of the book.

As I mentioned in the last chapter, I've noticed increasing numbers of young parents who not only seem to be lacking in In Charge skills but who also seem to not know they should possess them. In other words, some parents don't seem to understand the basic concept that parents *should* be the ones In Charge of children's behavior.

I would recommend to any of you who think you might be in this category that you actively try to be convinced of the concept. You could reread the first two paragraphs of this chapter, ask a number of people who've survived raising teenagers just how important they think it is for parents to be In Charge, or try out the concept while paying attention to how your child's behavior and your overall parenting experience improve. Actually, I would recommend doing all three...or anything else that has a chance of convincing you to be In Charge of your child *...right away!*

I'm going to give you some imagery to help you conceptually with being In Charge. I want you to imagine that on a centrally located wall in your home you have a large button that reads, *"Parent In Charge."* When it's in effect, it lights up. There are also two smaller buttons. One is called *"Unset,"* which is accessible by remote control to the parents and all children who are old enough to figure out how it works. The other button is called *"Reset"* and is operated by parental remote control.

A number of things—including a child defying a parent—cause the Unset button to be activated, and at least momentarily, the Parent In Charge light turns off. It is then the parent's job (without creating or allowing a power struggle and with as little fuss and emotion as possible) to quickly activate the Reset button and get that Parent In Charge light back on.

So you have a picture of the buttons in your mind: Parent In Charge, Unset, and Reset. It might be helpful for you to retain this imagined representation for when I further discuss this important concept.

In the rest of this chapter I will discuss and critique specific discipline techniques that I did or didn't find useful in being In Charge of children. First, I will extensively discuss one of my favorites.

I found the discipline technique of Counting my children to be an extremely effective way to restore compliance and hit the Reset button when they had done something to hit Unset. You know what the Counting Method is, I'm sure. I think it's been around for a very, very long time. It may even be programmed into our DNA—naaaaaw...probably not...well maybe.

Anyway, for generations Counting has been saving parents from most of the time having to get up off the couch in order to get compliance from children. Counting is the succinct and concise, instantly-understood-in-the-first-syllable numeric warning you give your children that conveys the important message that if they don't "listen up" and do what you said to do by the time you count to the "magic number" (which for me was zero, counting down from five), they will receive an immediate consequence. It only takes the statement of one or two numbers to get this message across. The Counting, by the way, should always be done in a firm and loving tone of voice.

I don't remember exactly in what period of my child-rearing I started using the Counting Method, but I think it was perhaps somewhere around the halfway point. So I can't say for sure how many children I actually used the method on. I do recall using it on my fourth, fifth, and sixth children as teenagers but I'm not sure if I used it on them as younger children and babies. I remember using it for sure from babyhood on with my last three children or so.

The amazing part of the Counting Method for me was always that I only had to issue the consequence a few times for each child as a baby and then never again—that is, with all of my children I used it on except the one who was severely oppositional defiant since soon after her birth. She was a different story. But even more amazing, now that I think of it, was that the children I used the method on starting somewhere in the middle of their upbringing, never needed a consequence even once.

When I Counted my non-oppositional-defiant children it was always easy to gain their compliance. This of course was after I had generally established with each child that (1) I was the person In Charge, and (2) when I Counted I always meant business (that is, I had become annoyed, frustrated, or angry enough with a child that I was determined to either get compliance or issue a consequence—their choice).

You definitely do have to save Counting for when you mean business. Or else there's a big risk you won't take action if a child actually allows you to reach the magic number (which sometimes happens). Not taking action when you Count a child to the magic number pretty much guarantees the Counting Method will not work for you. Consistency matters here. So don't use the Counting Method when you're not serious about enforcing compliance.

When you Count a child, you do have to be willing to get out of your chair or interrupt whatever you're doing and make a move towards the child. I usually started moving if the child didn't start complying before I got to number two or one. That's partly why I liked starting at number five. It gave the kids plenty of time to come out of their stubbornness and decide to comply before I had to get up or stop what I was doing and head their way. Sometimes my kids let me get to the point of moving towards them, whereupon they would usually be laughing and saying, "Okay, okay, okay." Once in awhile they would let me count to zero on my way towards them, but by the time I got there they were laughingly begging me to still let them comply, knowing that I would.

Again, if you're not willing with any particular incident to move towards the child upon Counting to your magic number, don't Count the child. If you're feeling too exhausted, lazy, or distracted, do something else. Perhaps make potentially idle threats, such as the following: "If you don't do what I told you to, I'm going to be massively unhappy about it for three-and-a-half days;" or, "If you don't listen up, you'll forever after have to wonder what you missed out on." These kinds of vague threats of revisiting the behavior at a later time allow you to do just that if you find yourself able to.

Whenever I could see that a child might be considering the fun of a two, one, or zero count, yet I was going to need more time to start moving, I would extend the Counting time by inserting fractions or extra vowels: "Two, one and a half, one, a half, a quarter, ooooone-eeeeeighth, zeeeeerooooo." This always delighted my children even more than regular Counting did.

I've never been able to figure out for sure why Counting was always an occasion for smirks and smiles with my older children (even the "Countee"). But there was typically kind of a party atmosphere after one of them had been Counted. One of my adult children recently verified that she always experienced a family Counting event as fun—which is kind of strange, if you think about it—Mom is ticked and insisting on compliance, and the children are complying against their will while being amused and having fun. Go figure. What mattered the most for me, though, was that Counting always induced compliance. I never once had to issue a consequence after the first few times with each baby.

Sometime after I'd been using the Counting Method with children for a number of years, I learned from another parenting advisor's book that Counting only works on "stop" behaviors, and that it doesn't work for "start" behaviors. Good thing I didn't know that when I first used the Counting Method because for me it worked just as well after directing my resistant child, "Start your homework" as it did with, "Stop watching TV."

Counting, I found, can even do stop and start simultaneously, as in, "Stop fooling around and start picking up your toys!" You don't actually have to say the words "stop" and "start" of course. You could just as easily get compliance with Counting after saying, "Turn off the TV," "Quit watching that stupid thing," or even, "I swear I'm going to throw that thing out the window some day!" You can also inspire compliance by Counting after communicating, "Do the dishes," or "Get to work," or "I've had it with this messy bedroom!" It's not about stopping or starting. It's about compliance in general and who is In Charge.

Another amazing thing about Counting is that it works equally well with sofa-strutting babies, bigger-than-yourself children, and everyone in-between. I swear it would still work on my adult children (themselves almost grandparents) if I ever needed it to. Counting, for me, was always an effective, quick, respectful, and mysteriously pleasant way to hit the Reset button.

The best and probably easiest time to teach children that you are the one In Charge is when they first start dishing out defiance. This can be as soon as they are able to crawl or walk along furniture and get into things (typically from six to ten months old). Of course, it's important to childproof a home so that dangerous things are out of reach, but there are always plenty of things kids simply have to learn not to touch, such as house plants, the dirt they're planted in, or computers.

When I first started raising children, the universally accepted means of teaching babies and toddlers not to touch off-limit things was the Slap The Hand Method. The initial step of this technique was to give the verbal warning, "No, no, touch!" when the baby got into something forbidden. When the baby did not comply, the warning was given again and the back of the touching hand was slapped hard enough to cause some physical discomfort or slight pain. This slap-accompanied admonition was to be repeated until the child obeyed.

I tried the Slap The Hand Method with my first child, or maybe two, but found it didn't work for me. The slaps always provoked the baby to anger and initiated power struggles between us—and I always clearly lost. The baby was always more stubborn about the touching than I was about the slapping and I always ended up just removing the child from the object like I could have done in the first place.

This method definitely didn't teach my baby to not touch off-limit items in the house, plus it caused some guilt on my part because I was not comfortable with inflicting the minor discomfort and causing that kind of anger. It could be suggested that this method did not work for me because of the excessively stubborn nature of my child. Not so. My first child, the only one I for sure remember trying the method on, was not stubborn by nature. In my opinion, the method itself provoked the stubbornness because it was mildly abusive.

The practice of distracting and removing babies from no-touch situations, of course, is only ever a temporary fix. It probably to some degree teaches them which items in the house are not to be touched, but it doesn't teach them to comply or to self-discipline. And it doesn't teach them solidly that the parent is In Charge. Babies can and do make their way back to intriguing items for more touching any time they choose, mostly when the parent is not watching.

I'm not exactly sure why the Slap The Hand Method endured through the years and was touted as a viable method to teach babies not to touch certain things. I don't remember ever actually observing the outcome of any other parent using the method. My guess is that if the method actually worked for some parents it may have done so because they persevered and issued harder and harder slaps until the baby gave up the battle of wills. I couldn't ever do that and don't advocate such. Actually, I don't advocate using the Slap The Hand Method at all because I don't think it's a respectful or functional way to try to teach early compliance.

But I did eventually develop a respectful method that successfully taught infants to comply with no-touch instructions. I'm not sure how or when I figured it out—it could have been as early as with my second child—but for sure I remember it working beautifully with my last three infants. (This discovery was obviously not the same kind of "aha" moment that some others in my life have been, or I would have remembered the occasion.) I do, however, have a general sense of using the method over a one or two decade period and only for sure failing to teach this kind of compliance to my first baby. But perhaps this is more wishful thinking than anything to do with memory. I apologize for the sketchiness of my recollection.

Using this new method did not feel to me like I was being abusive, did not provoke anger in my infants, and did not provoke power struggles between us. I can't remember if I initially used the method by itself, but I did ultimately use it in combination with the Counting Method. My guess is that I first started successfully using the Counting Method on school-aged children, and then I gradually used it on younger and younger kids until I was eventually dealing with infants who needed to learn about off-limit items in the home.

My discovery of the new method may have happened something like this: (1) a newly exploring, as yet untrained, pre-toddler infant touched a "no touch" item; (2) I issued a firm and loving "no touch" directive; (3) the infant, probably not yet even understanding English enough to know the meaning of "no touch," kept touching; (4) I again stated, "No touch" and started Counting the infant in a firm and loving tone of voice; (4) the infant, having no idea what the Counting Method was all about, kept touching the off-limit item; (5) having Counted down to zero, without obtaining compliance from the baby, I then had to come up with a functional consequence—but what?; (6) I pondered what consequence my young infant might be able to tolerate, understand, and be motivated by and decided on what I would try; and (7) I repeated the "no touch" message and gave the baby one firm pat on the cloth-diapered bottom—only just hard enough to hurt the pride a little and not hard enough to hurt the baby's bottom through the padding of the diaper.

No matter what had been the actual sequence of events that led to my learning the Pat The Diapered Bottom Method, the combined result of baby surprise and slightly wounded baby pride was always immediate compliance. The method was always effective. Sometimes there were a few self-nurturing baby tears. To this, I would respond by picking up the baby and giving empathetic hugs while reiterating a few more times the firm and loving no-touch admonitions.

The Pat The Diapered Bottom Method works just as well for teaching compliance when used without Counting. However, there must be some kind of verbal instruction or warning given at least once—but preferably a couple of times—in a firm and loving tone of voice. (Just like there needs to be some kind of verbal instruction before Counting.) **The verbal warning is what teaches the child to associate the pat with noncompliance in general and with not following the specific instructions in particular.**

The Pat The Diapered Bottom Method should not be used for anything other than noncompliant or defiant behavior. In other words, **it should not be used in response to a baby touching something prohibited if no immediately prior warning is given (even if the baby was warned in the past)**. There must be a warning of some kind that the baby is given in enough time to choose to ignore it (which is what constitutes defiance). Again, the pat on the diapered bottom should not be a consequence for touching something not allowed. It should only be a consequence for not heeding the parental warning and for current noncompliance.

Of course, the very first time or two that a baby or toddler is patted on the diaper for noncompliance, he or she does not know what the warning means or that the pat will be given. But it only takes a few times to learn all of this and become compliant in response to the warning. I only had to use this method of instruction a few times (only two to four pats for each baby). It taught them very quickly and easily that I was the one In Charge, and that when I did Count them or instruct them in a firm and loving tone of voice, they needed to comply right away. And this positive effect of the few pats per child lasted their entire childhood.

As I've said, the Pat The Diapered Bottom Method did not seem to provoke anger and never provoked power struggles. A number of things probably contributed to that, namely:

- The pat was not hard enough to cause physical pain through the diaper.
- Often my children's emotional reaction to the pat was self-nurturance and self-empathy (which they were proficient at by the age of six months or so).
- I added parental empathy.

- My babies had already been learning for months to trust me to have their best interests at heart, to be kind and nurturing to them, and to be parentally In Charge in a respectful way.

When I was a young teenager, my mother taught me the right way to spank children. Contrary to the norm of that era, she wasn't much of a spanker, except perhaps when the four of us were too young to remember. Nonetheless, for some reason, my mother thought it important to describe to me the least harmful way to spank children. She said that spanking a child should be done from below the child's bottom in an upwards motion, not horizontally from behind the bottom. Having been spanked as a child only once that I can remember—at which time I focused entirely on my innocence and not at all on the directional aspect of the spanking—I can't personally attest to the qualitative experiential difference between the two spanking directions.

My mother told me that spanking horizontally from directly behind a child had been deemed capable of damaging young kidneys. I never did happen upon any corroboration of this report. For all I knew it could have been simply an old wives' tale akin to "if you flip a kid over in the air you will 'flip' his liver over" yet it made sense to me. I imagine, though, that any such kidney damage would take much harder spanking than I could ever force myself to administer. I was generally opposed to inflicting even minor physical pain, let alone physical damage.

Anyway, when I did come up with the Pat The Diapered Bottom Method for teaching infants to comply, even though it was only just a few pats per infant, I always administered the pat in an upward motion to the more fleshy part of the bottom. It seems possible that since the bottom is a more fleshy body part than some others (and a fleshy-part pat might cause less pain or physical discomfort than a non-fleshy-part pat) that the recipient of the fleshy pat might experience less anger in response to it than would a recipient of a non-fleshy pat—especially since this particular fleshy body part in babyhood is usually accompanied by extra padding in the form of a diaper.

What I'm saying is that it is possible that this patting detail is somewhat relevant with this discipline method. The intent is not to physically hurt the baby. The intent is to slightly startle the child, to prevent a battle of wills, and to establish that the parent is the one In Charge.

Typical advice of decades ago was that a parent should never give empathy after disciplining a child because that would make it look like the parent was sorry for giving the discipline, which would essentially nullify its positive potential. I wholeheartedly disagree! I found that it was actually quite easy to give empathy for children's emotional states while not giving up my firm and loving position that compliance was required. It's actually quite easy to say, "I'm sorry you're upset, but I need you to stop touching the plant," or, "Poor baby, sad. No, no touch plant." I had very good results from combining empathy with firm and loving discipline.

I believe that teaching a very young child to be compliant disposes the child to be compliant not only in the immediate and short-term but also in general over the child's life (with other authority figures and with social expectations). Along with teaching children compliance, it's also very important to teach them assertiveness skills. This is so they won't submit to authority figures when inappropriate or unsafe to do so and so they can learn how to have their needs and wants met in life. About the same time I learned to get general compliance from my children, I also learned ways to teach them to be very assertive.

The techniques I used to teach them assertiveness involved:

- Giving simple encouragements for them to verbally express themselves.
- Not trying to shut down any negative emotions they respectfully expressed.
- Expecting and encouraging them to make their own age-appropriate decisions.

I much preferred having assertive children because I felt they were more able to function in life and survive in the world than unassertive children were. However, teaching my children to be assertive consistently came back to bite me when they developed into teenagers with Pre Adult Syndrome (PAS). For a year or two each, they occasionally asserted themselves towards me to the point of verbal aggression (for which I gave them consequences). In other words, they sometimes lipped off to me when they were angry about some decision I had made.

Of course, lipping off isn't all that uncommon for teenagers to do to parents even if they haven't deliberately been raised to be assertive. But, with children who've been assertive since toddlerhood, it's pretty much a guarantee. I survived it all however. And I believe my children came through the experience having learned to be respectfully assertive in life.

I'd like to say a few more things about the Pat The Diapered Bottom Method. My personal belief is that this method of teaching early and lasting compliance with parental authority is a very functional and beneficial technique that does not constitute physical violence or abuse. However, I understand that some parents may be opposed to using this method. They may believe or fear that it might actually physically hurt the child, that it might appear to hurt or be physically violent, or that it might somehow be emotionally abusive. I understand and respect those beliefs and fears. I come from a zero-tolerance-for-violence standpoint. As parents, we need to regularly question and monitor our own discipline practices and continually try to improve them because it's all too easy as a parent to justify abusive practices.

It's preferable, in my opinion, to use a method that effectively teaches babies at the very beginning of their trial noncompliance that the parents are the ones In Charge. I was never able to do that by verbal means alone. In my experience, a verbal assertion or warning for the first few noncompliant episodes with an infant is not enough of a consequence to establish the parent as being In Charge.

If anyone else has discovered any non-physical method that respectfully, lovingly, quickly, easily, and lastingly teaches infants for their entire childhood that the parent is In Charge, I would love to hear about it. Just because the Pat The Diapered Bottom Method was the best method I came up with, does not mean it's the only method or the best method ever to be found. However, I do believe it to be a very functional and respectful discipline method to use with infants.

There are obviously other ways to teach children that parents are In Charge. I certainly used something else before the Pat The Diapered Bottom Method; all of my children did know I was In Charge. Would I recommend using this method for parents who have post-infant children who don't yet know the parent is In Charge? Possibly, with caution if the child is already out of diapers. Or I would recommend tapping the child or giving a non-physical consequence.

I understand that the Pat The Diapered Bottom Method is not appropriate for childcare professionals to use on other people's children. Nor can it be used, even just the couple of times necessary, by parents (such as teen mothers) who are living in an institutional program that has a no-spank policy. This is because it has the *appearance* of spanking. The policies governing these kinds of childcare situations simply do not allow the use of such a method. I am all for nonviolent child rearing and non-physical disciplining, but I would like to make the point that disciplining issues aren't always black and white. Most of the time they are, but sometimes there are gray areas, with varying shades of gray. And there are various opinions and conclusions about the gray areas, even among professionals.

Here's a "gray" scenario I would like you to consider:

Let's take the case of Joey, a two-and-a-half-year old who has become a chronic, severe biter by the time he goes into foster care. For centuries, parents have been biting back their little biters, with great success in curtailing the biting. However, because of policies, that method cannot be used in foster care. Foster parents must understandably use a totally nonviolent parenting style.

So for many months, Joey severely injures other children in the foster home on an almost daily basis, typically giving them serious two-day bite marks. None of the approved consequences that are given him induce him to quit biting—not losing privileges, not two-minute timeouts—nothing. Many weeks of child therapy likewise does not cure him.

Eventually, an older child in the foster home takes matters into his own hands and tells Joey, "This is what it feels like to be bitten by you, and I'm going to do it every time you bite anyone." He then bites Joey—not quite as hard as Joey bites—but hard enough that Joey really doesn't like it.

Joey's biting habit disappears after only two of these instructive bites.

In this kind of scenario, there are two sides of the violence to consider—maybe one or two instructional, carefully placed, fairly hard bites to the biter versus hundreds or even thousands of randomly placed severe bites to other children. As well, if Joey is unstopped, there's the possibility that bite warfare could permeate the home and that the offender's behavior could escalate to even worse violence.

I'd just like to cover one last aspect of Counting. As I've said, Counting also worked very well in getting resistant teenage children to stop and start behaviors. But I can't definitively explain *why* it worked on teenagers. They certainly were not worried that I would pat their bottoms, and if they had really thought I might, they would not have stopped laughing for a very long time.

Part of the reason Counting worked with taller-than-me children may have been that I didn't do it all that often. It was not a daily occurrence. It was primarily used when I had no time or patience left for any other method. A last resort if you will.

Usually I would try other methods of gaining compliance before I Counted a child. For example, sometimes if children didn't comply fairly soon after being told to do something, I would help them up and help them get moving towards doing it. With an air of respectful no-more-nonsense authority I would gently lift and push them while trying to crack a joke and make them laugh.

Or if I had told children unsuccessfully to stop doing something, I might remove or confiscate whatever they were using to do it with while also trying to crack a related joke. Sometimes I would give warnings such as, "I'm getting angry about the garbage that has taken up residence in my kitchen," or, "This is the second time I'm telling you to hang up your coat, and I'm on the very verge of thinking up a consequence you most certainly will not like."

Years ago I bought a T-shirt that had a cute cartoon face with a fly on its nose and the words, "Stop bugging me." When I showed this new shirt with the novel slogan to my kids, they said, "Mom, that's nothing new. You say that all the time." Well, apparently I must have, although I've never heard me say it.

According to my children, I've often used those words to warn them that I was getting irritated with their behaviors. My point is that, prior to Counting, I usually gave my children other kinds of respectful preliminary promptings that gave them an opportunity to decide on their own to comply. These usually were enough for me to get compliance and hit the Reset button.

I always saved Counting for when there definitely would have been an "or else" had my children pushed me further. My tone and demeanor when Counting conveyed the message: I am the parent, and you are the child. Don't mess with me any more. I've totally had it with your behavior!

Although I don't believe I ever stated to my older children what the consequences would have been for them had I ever reached absolute zero (Counting to zero without them belatedly trying to comply) it most likely would have been the revoking of a privilege. I don't think my kids were particularly afraid of the possible consequences, or they would have shown some active concern over them. And having a privilege taken away was not a big, scary, unknown thing for them. So, I don't think Counting worked on teenagers because of any fear of me or the consequences.

Maybe Counting worked so well on teenagers partly because it had been working consistently since their baby days, and I had kept the Parent-In-Charge button lit up as regularly as possible right from Defiance Day One. Maybe it was because I had always tried hard to show respect for my children as human beings. And, as teenagers, whenever they knew they had pushed me to the point of Counting, they automatically kicked into compassion mode and showed some respect back. (Naaaaaw—not very likely—they were teenagers.) Maybe it was a combination of things that made Counting always work on my older children.

Come to think of it, some of the Counting episodes may, in fact, have been accidental or unexpected on the part of my children, due to me not always being one hundred percent consistent with sending out clear-cut warnings and "I'm getting bugged" cues. Or, depending on what was going on for me, I could sometimes jump from un-bugged to totally bugged in a flash, surprising them with a Counting.

So the kids may not have always intended to push me to the Counting point. They may have sometimes incorrectly thought they had another ounce of wiggle room before I would numerically enforce my parental authority—hence the surprised exchange of smirks. Hey! I just thought of something. Even more likely—maybe Counting was a form of family game they initiated when they were bored or something. (Along the lines of, "Let's see who can get away with the most without getting Counted.") That would ex-plain even better all those smirks!

Chapter Seven Summary: Being In Charge

- In order to prevent Type-Two Tantrums, it is super important that parents be In Charge of their children and not vice versa.

- Imagine that on a centrally located wall in your home you have a large button that reads, *"Parent In Charge."* When it is in effect, it lights up. There are also two smaller buttons. One is called *"Unset,"* which is accessible by remote control to the adults and children. The other button is called, *"Reset,"* which is operated by a parental remote control. A number of things can cause the Unset button to be activated, and at least momentarily the Parent In Charge light turns off. It is then the parent's job to somehow activate the Reset button and get the Parent In Charge light back on. You can use this imagery when dealing with your children.

- I found Counting my children to be an extremely effective way to restore compliance and hit the Reset button. Counting is the numeric warning you give your children that if they don't "listen up" and do what you said to do by the time you count to the "magic number" (which for me was zero, counting down from five), they will receive immediate consequences.

- The best and probably easiest time to teach children that you are the one In Charge is when they first start dishing out defiance (typically from six to ten months old).

- In combination with verbal "no touch" or other instructions, what I did find extremely effective as a consequence for reaching zero when I Counted a pre-toddler was giving one pat on the diapered bottom (only just hard enough to hurt the pride a little but not hard enough to hurt the baby's bottom through the padding). The combined result of surprise and slightly wounded pride was always immediate compliance.

- I only had to use this method of instruction a few times for each baby. The positive effect of the two to four pats per child lasted their entire childhood.

- My personal belief is that the Pat The Diapered Bottom Method of teaching early and lasting compliance with parental authority is a very functional and beneficial technique that does not constitute physical violence or abuse.

MegaMom's Wisdom for Tantrums

Chapter Eight: Time-outs and Groundings

I'm not sure exactly when I started using Counting to get my children to comply, but I believe it was long before Time-outs were invented and became the preferred North American method of discipline. Of course the Go To Your Room Method has probably been in use for as long as children have had their own rooms, but that's not the same thing as a Time-out. Even though Time-outs have been around long enough to have made it into the dictionary, and you probably know exactly what one is, I will clarify precisely what is typically meant by **Time-out.**

> **A *Time-out* is when a child misbehaves or won't comply and is removed from the situation and made to stand or sit still somewhere near the parent, usually for about one minute for each year of age.**

Oh, by the way, did you know the new invention is Time-ins? This means rewarding a child's positive behavior with positive time between parent and child. Apparently Time-ins became the preferred alternative for some people in recent years when it was finally discovered that Time-outs don't always work especially well.

Anyway, because I was already successfully using the Counting Method when Time-outs arrived on the parenting scene, I was not at all tempted to try them. But I've witnessed and studied probably hundreds of Time-outs in public places. One of the biggest reasons I'm not a fan of Time-outs is that they seem way more troublesome for the parent than for the child.

I think a good discipline system needs to be easy for the parent to use. It's excruciating for me even *watching* a

111

parent maintain a Time-out for four or five minutes (some-times with constant lecturing or reasoning attempts) while the child tries repeatedly to prematurely depart. I can only imagine how troublesome this discipline method must be for a busy parent to use numerous times a day. But for a five-year old who, say, forcefully smacked a sibling, five minutes is a cakewalk. It's five fun minutes of plotting his or her next move.

I think children's efforts to prematurely exit Time-outs are not necessarily based on wanting to *end* the Time-outs, so much as they are meant to annoy the parents. But Time-out parents (I've noticed) don't easily show annoyance. I'm not sure any of them still know how to even *feel* annoyance. They appear to have toughened, meditated, or prayed themselves into having "buckets" of unnatural patience. And this is exactly what it takes, in my opinion, to consistently use the Time-out Method.

It seems to me that many Time-outs are not much more than just timed power struggles, so I guess it's good in a way that they don't last more than a few minutes. Time-outs often fail miserably as a Reset tool because every time there's a wiggle towards escape, the child is hitting the Unset button. And when the parent pronounces the Time-out to be over (Reset), the child does not even wait for the whole pronouncement but runs away on the first word (Unset).

When Time-outs are *not* power struggles, because the child sits willingly on the chair or stands obediently at the wall for the whole time, they remind me so much of a discipline method used many decades ago. Children were routinely sat or stood in corners (with or without dunce caps). In my own elementary school days, I witnessed a few such public "corner occasions," without caps. The focus of that method always seemed to be more on the child than on the behavior and more on trying to motivate by humiliation

112

than by anything positive. The connotation (or even declaration) was not that the child's behavior was unacceptable but that the *child* was "bad." In my opinion that is mild emotional abuse. (I disagree, however, with those who think even occasionally telling a child that she or he is "good" is also abusive. I believe it would be the rare child under very rare circumstances that could be harmed by such a parental message as that.)

Somewhat similar to putting children in corners, Time-outs seem to put unnecessary focus on the child and inadequate focus on the child's behavior. In my more current observations of willing wall huggers, however, to the credit of the parents, I've never noticed any of them intentionally connoting that their child was bad. There must be a *Time-outs for Intellectuals* Manual out there somewhere because these Time-out parents are *good*! However, because the focus is on the child standing or sitting—sometimes in a public place and quite often with an audience of strangers— I think it would be amazing if the child did not self-attribute or self-connote "badness" to some degree.

All of the above was enough for me to not use Time-outs. However, there's even more. Consequences for children seem to work best if they logically fit with the infraction. They work even better if they are "natural" (meaning not artificially instituted by parents) but rather, dished out by the laws of nature. Here are some examples of natural, versus fitting and unfitting consequences :

- **Scenario One.** A child is told to put her allowance in her piggy bank but chooses to put it in her pocket and loses it at play. With such "natural" consequences there is absolutely no call for parental discipline. It's already done.

- **Scenario Two.** The child has agreed to save half of his allowance every week in order to buy souvenirs on the upcoming family vacation, but he spends one whole week's allowance on candy. Nature is not involved here, so the parent feels a need to discipline. Preferably the consequences should match the offense.

  o **Fitting consequences.** If the child was very young, he could get extra help with managing his next week's allowance, having to save one hundred percent of it for the vacation trip and not getting prior access to it. If he was older, he could simply have less souvenir money to spend on the trip, no matter how much begging he does.

  o **Unfitting consequences.** Grounding the child for a week would be an unsuitable consequence. Taking away social freedoms would be an over-prescription and would not match the specific infraction of not saving money for an agreed-upon expenditure.

I've tried to think of a circumstance when it would be a fitting or logical consequence to stand a child at a wall, as is done with Time-outs. I've thought hard, expecting that with the wide variety of misbehaviors my children have subjected me to, I should be able to come up with an oh-you-*so*-need-to-stand-at-the-wall type of offense. But I can't. Any wall-related offenses I can remember usually involved felt pens and crayons and such, and I thought it more logical and fitting to expect the child to remove the art work rather than stand and admire it.

Likewise, I hardly ever sat children on chairs as a consequence for their actions. I believe the only occasions I ever placed and watched my children on chairs for a specified amount of time was as a follow-up consequence for their outrageous behavior during seated public events we had attended as a family. But their consequence was not simply to sit on the chairs. They also had to be relatively quiet and still as they should have been (but were not) at the events. And the amount of time for the consequence was similar to the real time of the event, not one measly minute per year of age. Also, if my children misbehaved during their consequence time, I started the clock over again.

In this circumstance, if I had given my children a six- or eight-minute-long consequence for an hour of giving me grief, I believe they would have perceived their fun as worth their trouble and been quite prepared to do it again. Instead, receiving consequence time equal to their misbehavior time (with a few restarts) caused them to not want to repeat the offense.

I know that in some circles (including some Government Child Welfare jurisdictions) it's seriously considered punishable child abuse to consequence more than one minute of Time-out per year of age (this is The One-Minute Rule). A two-year old supposedly is only capable of tolerating and learning from a two-minute Time-out, and so on. But it seems to me that a two-year old who hurts someone on purpose—and doesn't get sent to her room or something for maybe ten minutes—isn't getting a strong enough no-violence message. One minute of Time-out per year of age is entirely inadequate when used with more serious offenses or with children who are old enough to calculate when the inconvenience or discomfort of a consequence is worth the fun of the behavior—potentially from the age of two and up.

I'm not trying to traumatize anyone here, but I'm going to give a few examples of some more serious childhood offenses (that your children will hopefully never commit). I want to be able to clearly make my point because there are families that have been negatively affected by agencies' adoption of the Time-Out with the One-Minute Rule as the only acceptable method of child discipline. Consider the following:

- An eight-year old maliciously tries to push her babysitter down a flight of stairs. Is eight minutes of Time-out an adequate consequence?
- A four-year old does the same thing. Is four minutes of Time-out enough?

- A twelve-year old deliberately and maliciously destroys a brother's new iPod. Is twelve minutes of consequence enough?
- What if a three-year old does the same thing just as deliberately and maliciously? Should the One-Minute Rule be applied here?

No, no, no to all of the above! Of course not! The One-Minute Rule is ludicrous when applied to more serious behavior problems—and to children older than a toddler.

In order to further argue this important point, I am going to make some more comparisons.

Consider the following. As parents, we do not generally raise children in isolation from society. We raise children who are expected to function *in* society and follow the social rules. Teens and adults who have not yet learned to follow the rules and regulations of society and who get caught committing a crime or violation typically go through the justice system. Think, if you will, how our society consequences teens and adults for their crimes.

Offenders usually receive stiff consequences. Even a first offense often nets a criminal hundreds of dollars in fines, dozens of hours in community service, or months in

116

jail time, in addition to a permanent criminal record (for adults). None of this, of course, is remotely similar to fifteen minutes (for a fifteen-year old) or thirty minutes (for a thirty-year old) of sitting on a chair or standing in a corner. Social consequences for criminal offenses are huge. Consequences dictated by the One-Minute Rule for children are miniscule.

Can you imagine how motivating a speeding ticket would be for a fifty-year old if the associated consequence was to sit on a chair for fifty minutes instead of getting driver's license points and a hefty fine that hurt the pocketbook? Not very, I'm sure. A child's type of Time-out like this could not possibly motivate adult speeders in general to slow down, and especially so if speed traps were relatively rare. As well, a sixty-year old drunk driver or accident-causing drunk driver would need monumentally more motivation than a restriction to a chair for one hour in order to transform into a safe driver.

Another important type of consequence that typically is very unlike the One-Minute prescription is the natural consequence. If a child decided to step into traffic, knock the paint can over, not study for a test, light something on fire, knock over the wasps' nest, or leave the tricycle directly behind the car, there most likely would be a natural negative outcome that would be much more severe than anything stemming from the One-Minute Rule.

Consequences received by children between infancy and adulthood, in general, need to gradually and steadily increase in duration, toughness, or intensity. This motivates the steady rate of behavioral learning that fully prepares children for adult functioning by the time they reach adulthood. At every age children need to receive functional consequences for their misdeeds. A functional consequence, by my definition, is one that effectively nullifies the benefit

117

that is earned through the commission of the offense. In other words, the benefit of the crime isn't worth the bother of the consequence.

So imagine for a minute that I've convinced you that the One-Minute Rule is not appropriate for serious offenses and for older children, but you still believe it should be used for young children. I ask you, then, at what childhood age or severity of offense does the One-Minute Rule start to become dysfunctional? When should it be discarded? Good questions.

By now you know, of course, that I'm not at all a fan of Time-outs—with or without the One-Minute Rule. You might have surmised that I say we throw out the One-Minute Rule altogether. I do, in fact. However, to parents who insist on using it with their children, I would recommend throwing it out for sure by the time they are three. In other words, I can only really see it maybe, possibly having *some* benefit in application to slightly misbehaving two-year olds (and really only then if combined with a consequence more fitting than sitting on a chair or standing at a wall).

I recommend that parents establish the duration of logical consequences on an incident-by-incident and child-by-child basis—other than for things that make sense to have a standard consequence, such as losing the use of a bicycle for a week for leaving it in the driveway. I know it probably sounds pretty daunting and overwhelming to have to set consequences incident by incident, especially for novice parents. Perhaps it's even more daunting, though, for those who've devotedly followed the standard Time-out timetables since the beginning of their parenting careers. However, on-the-spot consequence setting isn't really that difficult to master.

I assure you it only takes a few dozen smirks from your children to be secure in the knowledge that you haven't been meting out severe enough consequences or long enough

Groundings. And it only takes a few dozen earsplitting wails to be certain that your consequences are too severe or your Groundings are too long. Like with anything else, the more you practice trying to make a consequence fit the offense both in type and duration, the better you will get. Also, your child's reaction—that is somewhere in between a smirk and a wail—will validate your success.

The reason I say that the One-Minute Rule is only good for two-year olds (and not for younger children) has nothing, really, to do with the One-Minute Rule. It has to do with another Time-out issue that I have: babies under a year and a half or so are too young to be disciplined by this method. Yet babies by six to ten months old need to be taught that parents are In Charge.

Forcing a ten-month-old baby to sit still for one minute because of defiantly ripping a plant, for instance, has absolutely no chance of teaching anything. You could *tell* the baby why you are making her sit on the chair, but she would not understand in the least, even if you were the best mime talent in town. Such a consequence is too delayed and too unrelated to the offense. It's also beyond the baby's functioning ability, which makes it totally unenforceable. (Have you ever tried to make a ten-month old sit on a chair or stand at a wall for even half a minute?)

Any natural or logical consequence that could possibly fit with the offense of ripping a plant would also be too delayed and way beyond the functioning of a ten-month old. But an immediate surprise pat to the diapered bottom after a couple of firm and loving verbal warnings, delivered *during* the noncompliant act, can and does teach—in just a few episodes.

Of course, the pat is not meant to be a logical consequence of ripping the plant leaf. It is a logical consequence of the child defying the parent. It is the parent interrupting the child's defiant behavior, saying in effect, "I am In

Charge and you are expected to listen to me." Even babies as young as six months old are capable of choosing to behave compliantly when taught by just a few episodes of this combination of firm and loving verbal warnings, non-abusive assertion of parental authority, and perhaps some empathy.

Children don't usually have the mobility (and hence the opportunity) to defy parents a whole lot until six to ten months of age. However, I believe even younger children than six-month olds can comprehend and learn compliance if exposed to this firm and loving teaching process. A personal experience convinced me of this.

At four months of age, with obviously no malicious intent, one of my babies bit me very hard without warning when I was breastfeeding him. Without thinking, my automatic reaction was to sharply smack his small cheek with my fingertips (not hard enough to leave a mark or injure him but hard enough to startle him). He then released his bite and I pushed firmly down on his lower jaw and shouted, "No bite!" I'm sure he was surprised and maybe frightened by the tap on his cheek, the pressure on his jaw, and the louder-than-average communication. I think he cried. If he did, I would have given him empathy.

This little four-month-old baby refused to breastfeed for the rest of that day. But he did accept the bottle (which he was familiar with). He never bit me again in the eight additional months that I breastfed him. This proves (I believe) that he was able to associate his unintentionally hurtful behavior with my unpleasant reaction and to consciously not repeat his behavior. I've known breastfeeding mothers whose babies regularly bite them late into the first year (babies that receive no consequences for the biting). My experience convinced me that a four-month old typically has the *ability* to learn compliance, if not generally the *need*.

120

I recently witnessed the Timing-out of a child in a restaurant. He was probably four years old. The mother stood him up and faced him to a wall because he had not stopped playing with the sugar packets on the table after she had once told him not to. She stood by him for four minutes or so while he repeatedly tried to escape back to his chair.

If I had been this parent, instead of simply telling the child not to play with the packets, I probably would have started out giving a few neutral reasoning statements. The main purpose of this technique is that it doesn't generally thrust children (or adults for that matter) into "challenge mode" like direct orders easily can. No one prefers to be ordered around, so if there's a more respectful and successful way to communicate, why not use it? In this circumstance, I would have said to the child such things as: "Those packets are for people who drink coffee and tea. Those aren't for children to play with, so please don't, sweetheart."

If neutral statements and a respectful request didn't work in this case—although they usually do—I probably would have calmly taken the packets out of the child's reach. I would have then reiterated, firmly and matter-of-factly, the non-confrontational statement, "Those aren't for kids to play with." This is all it would take to Reset. Voilà!—A battle-free solution. Parent In Charge. (However, if the child did not tolerate the removal of the packets and threw a tantrum, that would require further action on the part of the parent.)

It's very important for parents to remember that a child does not have to willingly and overtly comply for a parent to get back In Charge in such a situation. The parent does not have to "win" by having the child concede. The parent only has to successfully end the child's undesirable behavior. The solution does not need to incorporate any kind of battle, and it's far better if it doesn't. In my opinion,

Time-outs (by their very confrontational essence) almost guarantee the child will slip into power struggle or challenge mode.

Over the next nine pages or so, I would like to share my thoughts on the discipline technique of Grounding. I think Grounding can be very useful as a discipline method when it fits the offense. One fitting example is when a child is being abusive to other children, and she gets to spend some alone time in her bedroom (the go-to-your-room variety of Grounding). Another is when a teen or preteen doesn't come home by curfew, and he gets to stay home and miss out on the next few social events (the you're-not-going-anywhere sort of Grounding).

To be beneficial, however, Groundings have to be of the exactly perfect duration. This can be really, really tricky. I'm not kidding. And getting the right duration is especially critical if Groundings have been the standard or primary consequence for most of the child's offenses, constituting overuse in the eyes of the child. Groundings have to be long enough but short enough to produce a reaction somewhere in between the following:

1. The child feeling the benefit was definitely worth the consequence.
2. The child detesting your innards.

A couple of examples of the benefits being worth the consequences could be (1) five minutes of delightful pestering of a sibling generating five minutes of bedroom incarceration, and (2) one fun evening two hours late for curfew yielding one evening of Grounding. On the opposite end, consequences that could cause the child to hate parental innards might be (1) five minutes of delightful pestering yielding two hours of bedroom incarceration, and (2) two hours late for curfew netting two weeks of Grounding.

The tricky part of issuing Groundings is that there's practically no space to work with in between the long enough and short enough of them. I ultimately developed a personal formula that helped me wedge between these Grounding guideposts of short enough and long enough. If the offense was not of a serious nature, and if there was a duration aspect to it, I would prescribe a Grounding of two to three times the duration of the offense. I called this The 2-3X Principle.

For example, if a child was disruptive and disrespectful for five minutes in the kitchen, a ten or fifteen minute bedroom stint was appropriate and not too harsh. Five minutes would not be tough enough, and twenty minutes would be too tough—unless the offense was of a more serious nature or was recurrent.

It goes without saying that bedroom Groundings must be given without access to games, computers, toys, books, etc. If the bedroom environment is essentially too fun or entertaining for Groundings, then an alternate location could be found—perhaps the laundry room would work. This approach is typically easier than ensuring denied access to the fun things during Groundings in the bedroom.

Grounding can be a very beneficial tool, but it's one that should be used sparingly, like Counting. My theory is that Groundings—and the revoking of privileges in general—if they're of an effective duration, create a mild residue of anger for the Grounded child. Ideally, this child anger should dissipate at least a little bit before another batch is produced. Cumulative child anger of this sort is not a good thing, even when the child's behavior warrants the consequences that generate the anger. Of course, sometimes the child gives the parent no choice but to issue consecutive or nearly consecutive Groundings because Groundings are the

most natural consequences (for curfew violations for example). However, alternatives to Grounding and the revoking
of privileges should at least be examined at such times.

My experience has been that Grounding teenagers
excessively (either too often or for too long) usually creates
exceptional, outstanding, and incessant power struggles
(otherwise known as mutiny). Before they are solved, such
states of mutiny usually spread within the family to include
every sibling old enough to empathize with the overly-
grounded teen. These situations are extremely difficult to
deal with and fix once they get started. Needless to say, I'm
not a fan of long or frequent Groundings.

I've occasionally heard, via my teens, about friends of
theirs who were Grounded for the entire summer. The two-
or three-month Grounding was always for a medium-level
curfew or rule violation, such as taking the car somewhere
without permission or getting caught with cigarettes. In my
opinion, such long Groundings are extremely inappropriate.
My children were always mortified that such lengthy
Groundings were even legal.

My teens reported to me that their friends actually
tolerated these summer-long Groundings, without mutiny,
albeit with a definite loss of enthusiasm for life. I pondered
why these teens passively tolerated such extreme Groundings. I'm thinking they most likely hadn't developed strong
assertiveness skills. Also, their parents were obviously fairly
controlling. The teens probably understood their parents'
dual, co-determination to quash, with even harsher consequences, any attempted backlash to the Groundings. And
perhaps these teens did not have a plentitude of old-enough
siblings willing to risk alignment in a solid wall of mutiny
against the parents.

Ultimately, the parents in these summer-long
Grounding scenarios likely perceived the length of the
Groundings as appropriate and justifiable because the

children probably never repeated the offenses. *But at what expense* did the parents gain compliance in these situations? Breaking the children's spirits? Causing long-term parental hatred? Adding preventable items to the what-I-hated-about-how-you-raised-me list for later expression in early adulthood? The compliance was probably enforced at the expense of all of the above, I'm guessing. I can not think of a circumstance in which a summer-long Grounding would ever be appropriate—except possibly for the child's safety—but then that wouldn't be a Grounding, technically.

As I mentioned earlier, Groundings should not be used if they do not fit the offense. It is not logical to restrict all social outings for the whole summer for taking the car once without permission. The logical and fair consequence for that offense would be to take away the freedom of using the car for a number of times and to remove the privilege and trust of having unsupervised access to the car keys.

After many years of figuring out how to Ground teens effectively, I discovered a way to improve the process. I learned how to reduce the teens' automatic anger at being Grounded and my automatic frustration and anger with the situations, also. It was probably one of my teens that came up with the concept, eagerly suggesting she do some chore for me in lieu of her Grounding. I learned that it works well to let children work off *some* (but not all) of their Grounding time by voluntarily doing extra chores. In my experience, most Grounded children will volunteer in this way, if given the option. This system helps both parties reduce anger and increase a sense of needs being met, justice, fairness, vindication, and goodwill.

Many years ago I developed a system for myself that standardized the Grounding process (Grounding Standardization Method). I needed to use this system during a few episodes when I had more than one child at a time in persistent curfew-violation status. These were teens who were in Pre Adult Syndrome (PAS) mode who erroneously thought they were old enough, mature enough, capable enough, and wise enough for total self-management—hence their determination to consistently self assert. These children were aligned with each other, ignoring the realities that (1) they were not legally of age, (2) they still lived in *my* home, and (3) that *I* was still going to be the one In Charge. (This is the kind of situation I was referring to earlier when I said that teaching my children to be assertive from a very young age usually came back to bite me when they were teenagers in PAS mode.)

This Grounding system was very helpful in standardizing Groundings for one child (from one time to the next) but even more so between children, to eliminate accusations of unfairness against me. This two-part method included keeping a handy list of child privileges (divided into levels) on the side of the refrigerator or on the inside of a kitchen cabinet door. The list always included the following:

GROUNDING STANDARDIZATION METHOD

Grounding Levels
(Loss of Privileges)

- Level 1: Going with friends.
- Level 2: Having friends over.
- Level 3: Using the telephone.
- Numerous other Levels that were to do with the use of television and other electronic devices and such. [These could include children's personal possessions, even ones they had purchased for themselves with their own money.]

126

- Various other Levels that were for when severe restrictions were needed. These included the activities and things I really wanted my children to have, such as lessons, use of bicycles for transportation, doors on their bedrooms, desserts, and employment (for the older children).

At the bottom of this list, I declared, "Unless otherwise stated, all Groundings include only the loss of Levels One and Two privileges." In the list I included any and all privileges that I might consider removing from children if their behavior warranted it. I did not list privileges that I would generally be unwilling to remove (for whatever reason).

Whenever I issued a Grounding sentence, I stated (1) how long it would be for; and (2) if it was other than Level 2, what Level the Grounding was. I decided the level of the Grounding based on the infraction details and the level of annoyance the child's behavior had generated in me. For instance, if the child was very late returning from a friend's house, I was most likely to Ground to Level Three (taking away telephone privileges so the child would have temporarily reduced contact with the friend). However, I would likely increase the Grounding to a higher level if the child's lateness badly interrupted my functioning or my sleep. For example, if I had to go look for the child or look for the child after my bedtime, I would be inclined to Ground at a higher level than otherwise. Groundings at the highest levels were usually only issued during situations of mutiny.

The second part of my Grounding Standardization Method was a Grounding Factors Point System. This is what made it possible to standardize the duration of Groundings. Previously, it had been difficult to know if I for sure was being fair, what with multiple factors and personalities involved, so I wasted time vacillating between different lengths of Groundings before I could decide on one. And I still got: "Darla's Grounding was shorter, and she was later than I was! Not fair!" But the new system prevented such accusations and disputes about unfairness on my part.

It was a big relief for me to no longer feel intimidated by those inevitable accusations of unfairness. I no longer had to pre-plot how I would defend my decision when handing it out. (I suspect those of you who scoff at me for having been intimidated by my own teenagers have no experience in handling, singlehandedly, two or more resolute, conspiring, assertive, allied pre-adults who stop at very little in their all-out joint effort against you to be self-managed. I would just like to say that I hope you never have to go there.)

Anyway, my Grounding Factors Point System changed the dynamics of these situations, and I was thereafter able to confidently issue Grounding sentences without the anticipation of a barrage of complaints. In fact, there weren't even *token* complaints. It was wonderful! There may actually have been some muttered ones. However, by that time in my parenting career, I had already acquired the very useful skill of responding to under-the-breath comments from my children by happily ignoring them. So, I didn't notice murmurings—if there were any.

Another benefit of my Grounding Factors Point System (had my children ever cared to take advantage of it) was that they could actually personally pre-calculate, prior to committing planned curfew offenses, exactly how long their Groundings would be for. They could also calculate whether or not the Groundings would conflict with any of their important upcoming events or weekend plans and then adjust, downgrade, or cancel the planned offense accordingly. (I never caught any of my children taking advantage of this built-in feature of my Grounding Standardization Method, and none ever admitted to using it.) But ideally (I hoped) this awareness benefit would have inspired better decisions in my children.

My Grounding Factors Point System chart was like the following—[explanatory comments are in brackets]:

GROUNDING STANDARDIZATION METHOD

GROUNDING FACTORS:

- Each point equals one six-hour period of Grounding. [For my purposes these were clock hours, including sleeping time.]

TIME FACTORS:
- 3 points for every hour involved [in the offense].

RESPONSIBILITY FACTORS:
- 1 point – Failing to leave appropriate information. [e.g., I didn't know where the child was.]
- 1 point – Failing to negotiate the time. [The child did not ask when to be home.]
- 1 point – Failing to call when agreed upon or when appropriate.
- 1 point – Failing to call about change of activities or locations.
- 1 point – Failing to honor a commitment.
- 1 point – Inconveniencing another person or other people.
- 1 point – Causing another person or people to fear for your safety.
- 1 point – Requiring another person or people to have to track you down.
- 1 point – Leaving a medium amount of chores undone.
- 1 point – Failing to check in when arriving home.
- 1 point – Premeditating.
- 1 point – Committing a repeat offense of a similar nature.
- 2 points – Leaving lots of chores undone.
- 2 points – Leaving chores undone that someone else had to do.

- 2 points – Going against the rules for the home.
- 2 points – Going somewhere after explicit instructions not to.
- 2 points – Going somewhere when already Grounded.
- 3 points – Necessitating police intervention [e.g., I had to report the child as missing.]

ACTIVITY FACTORS:
- 1 point – School- or church-related.
- 1 point – Something usually allowed with permission.
- 2 points – Something usually not allowed.
- 3 points – Something always prohibited.

HONESTY FACTORS:
- 1 point – Lying to manipulate or cover up.
- 2 points – Coming clean only after investigation, or not coming clean at all.

OTHER FACTORS:
- Other factors may arise and will be graded at the time of occurrence.

Using this system was easy. I just added up all of the points that applied and then multiplied them by the number of hours of Grounding per point. For example, a child who was one hour late coming home, failed to call home to discuss a change of location (I had called Jimmy's house to find out he and Jimmy had gone to Bart's house), and failed to check in when he arrived home would have racked up five points at six hours per point, for a total of thirty hours of Grounding.

What wasn't easy for me was remembering, days later, exactly when children would be off their Groundings. I found it very helpful to write the dates and Grounding release times on my calendar. Whenever a child conveniently or even genuinely forgot about being Grounded and got my permission to go somewhere before the Grounding was over, I could easily go back and calculate the extended release time and penalty. (I assigned to the Grounded children the duty of remembering the Groundings and refraining from asking me to go anywhere or partaking of any prohibited activities during them.)

If parents do decide to use a Grounding Factors Point System such as this, they should customize it to their own situations, preferences, and priorities, keeping in mind the key principle of staying In Charge in a respectful way. Of course, the factor values and Grounding time for each point should also be customized to each family. And the chart items and values should be formally adjusted whenever needed in order to keep the desired child reactions somewhere between smirks and wails.

As I said, I only used this kind of system a few times when I had multiple curfew violators who were complaining about inconsistent and unfair Grounding times between siblings. However, I can't see the harm in using a system like this with only one curfew violator, or introducing it at the very hint of a child's curfew-violation habit.

Chapter Eight Summary: Time-outs and Groundings

- A Time-out is when a child is removed from a misbehavior situation and made to stand or sit still somewhere near the parent, usually for about one minute for each year of age.
  - Time-outs seem way more troublesome for the parent than for the child.
  - It takes "buckets" of unnatural patience to consistently use the Time-out Method.
  - Time-outs are not much more than timed power struggles.
  - Time-outs often fail miserably as a Reset tool.
  - Time-outs are not a natural or fitting kind of consequence.
  - Time-outs sometimes give the connotation of "bad child."
  - Time-outs don't work with defiant infants (they are too young to understand the consequence).
  - The One-Minute Rule is dysfunctional for kids older than two and for more serious childhood misbehavior.
  - A functional consequence is one that effectively nullifies the benefit earned through the commission of the offense. Time-outs don't do this.
  - Parents should establish logical consequences on an incident-by-incident and child-by-child basis.

- Groundings can be very useful when they fit the offense and when they are of the exactly perfect duration.

- My personal formula to help me wedge between the short and long guideposts for Groundings: The 2-3X Principle.

- Grounding can be a very beneficial tool, but it's one that should be used sparingly.

- My two-part Grounding Standardization Method helps standardize Groundings for one child (from one time to the next) and between children (to eliminate accusations of unfairness).

MegaMom's Wisdom for Tantrums

Chapter Nine: Other Consequences and Parenting Techniques

In the last chapter I discussed how neutral statements can help gain the compliance of young children. Parents do well to develop useful repertoires of versatile neutral statements that they can use as substitutes for confrontational direct orders. (Don't get me wrong. Direct orders are sometimes perfectly acceptable and even advisable, such as: "No bite!" or "Get off the road! Now!" or "Get that kite away from the power line!" or "Don't let the snake out!") But neutral statements can also come in very handy.

Here are some ideas to get you started:

- "Children are expected to be quiet in restaurants"—as opposed to—"Be quiet!"
- "When kids are quiet in vehicles, the driver has a much better chance of driving safely"—as opposed to—"Be quiet so I can drive!" (Although there certainly are perilous times when, "Quiet!" is indicated.)
- "Milk that gets put back in the fridge right away has a lot better chance of not going sour"—as opposed to—"Put the milk away!"
- "Beds are not for jumping on"—as opposed to—"Stop jumping on the bed!"
- "Chandeliers are not for swinging on"—as opposed to—"Get down from there!"
- "Goldfish are not for swallowing"—as opposed to—"Don't swallow that fish!"

Just kidding about the chandelier and the goldfish—those two situations are more in need of direct orders than neutral statements. Plus, seasoned parents all know they

135

would never get an opportunity to say *any* goldfish statements to their children because goldfish-swallowing incidents only ever come to light when it is much too late to
intervene on behalf of the goldfish—sometimes not until
decades later. (Decades later is typically when parents are
most likely to learn of the most offensive, embarrassing, and
life-threatening things their children ever did. This is also
when many cold-case child-rearing mysteries are finally
solved.)

I'd like to add a few more thoughts about consequences and how they should "fit." Besides making consequences fit the offenses of your children, it also helps to
make each consequence fit the offender. In other words, if
you're going to take away a privilege from a child, make
sure it's a privilege that the child cares about losing. It's
really rather pointless to confiscate something or remove a
privilege the child could care less about. The ideal thing or
privilege to confiscate is not likely the same for every child
or necessarily the same for any child from one day to the
next.

It is very important for parents to remember that
many children quickly figure out the confiscation system
well enough to (1) say they don't care about a privilege that
they very much do, and (2) say they do care about a privilege they really don't. Children often hope to trick us into
taking away the wrong privilege. If you find yourself sus-
pecting that you've been duped in this manner, and the
withdrawal of the target privilege is having no detectible
effect, it is perfectly acceptable to unilaterally declare a
switch in privilege withdrawal (without, of course, accusing
the child of trickery—a highly impossible situation to prove,
due to legitimate, ongoing fluctuations in childhood focus).

You've probably been admonished by some parenting
professional or other to never change your verdict after

you've issued a consequence to a child. What malarkey! It's perfectly acceptable to occasionally revisit and increase a consequence, advising the offender: "Oh, by the way, when I said you weren't going to get any dessert or treats for a week because of eating all of the Halloween candy I was going to hand out, I wasn't thinking clearly. It's going to be *two* weeks. *And* you won't be getting your allowance for two weeks."

On the other hand, if you belatedly realize the consequence you gave was too harsh, modify it and tell your child you think you made a mistake: "You know when I said I wasn't going to let you hang out with your friends for a week because of getting home twenty minutes late from the game the other day? I think that was a little stiff and I'm going to change it to three days." It's also quite acceptable and often preferable to delay issuing a verdict until "later" (especially if you're too angry at the time of the offense and don't have a readymade, pre-planned consequence). This is, of course, as long as you remember to do it later—most of the time.

Sometimes parents feel desperate to motivate their children to accomplish some generalized parental ideal (such as always doing their chores willingly) or some distant lofty parental goal (such as graduating with a 4.0 GPA). Desperate parents often come up with threats of some unfitting consequence for children's noncompliance with their own generalized ideals or lofty goals (for example, no Christmas or birthday gifts, or not going with the family on vacation). Desperate parents also sometimes offer big enticing rewards to their children for accomplishment of parental hopes and dreams (for example, a new sports car).

My recommendation to parents is don't do either of these. Why? Number one, offering your kids big enticing rewards for accomplishment of your dreams puts too much pressure on them for the wrong reasons—it's better if kids are working on accomplishing their own dreams, with your support and understanding for their difficulties and struggles that are inevitable. Number two, it doesn't work to threaten big, unfitting consequences; but if you do you will look and feel like the biggest, baddest meanie, and you will have to eat your words or actually *be* the biggest, baddest meanie.

Why, you ask, do such big and wonderful rewards and such big or scary threats not motivate kids to do what you want them to? I'm not exactly sure. But kids (just like adults) are mostly incapable of being motivated in general by such threats of loss or promises of gains that are not logically and immediately connected to their daily actions, choices, and personal goals. Perhaps the reason these motivators don't work for accomplishing big, generalized goals is related to the reason why most people who make New Year's resolutions usually fizzle on them before February. (I was one of those fizzlers until I stopped tormenting myself with making resolutions, which mostly had been unrealistic and unattainable under my circumstances.)

It also helps a whole lot when dishing out consequences to have them thought up ahead of time. There is a two-part reason for this. Firstly, parents can do a better job of coming up with fitting consequences when they're cool, calm, and rational (and not in the middle of feeling victimized and enraged by the child's behavior). I recommend that parents brainstorm, in writing, all possible consequences for all anticipated offenses and then choose the best and fairest predetermined consequence for each offense. These could even be posted somewhere for the children to freely ponder on—as long as it is clearly stated that these are the "likely" or "possible" consequences. This would allow the parents to easily upgrade or downgrade the consequences as warranted.

The second part of the reason for thinking up consequences ahead of time is that this can allow parents to
totally, altogether avoid getting angry with children's behaviors. Here's an example for you. Imagine that you pull
into your driveway that is blocked by a tricycle or bicycle.
You've pre-decided that such items will be confiscated and
hung up in the garage for x amount of time. So you calmly
get out of your vehicle, hang up the trike or bike, move your
vehicle into the garage, walk into the house, and respectfully and lovingly notify the child of the confiscation. Voilà—
an anger-free incident. Well, anger-free for you that is. The
child will likely be somewhat angry about having the tricycle hung up (especially if x amount of time equals "too
harsh" in the child's mind).

I'm sure most parents can readily compare such a
pre-determined-consequence scenario to actual situations of
their own when they didn't have a pre-thought-up consequence, and they completely lost their tempers. This kind of
contrast readily demonstrates that not having a readymade
consequence is what allows a parent to slip into feeling
helpless, victimized, and angry. Having a handy consequence already figured out is what makes the parent feel
strong, rational, In-Charge, and prepared to deal fairly with
the situation.

When children break family and social rules, it's important that they be the ones to experience the anger and
not the parents. If the parents typically feel all of the anger
or more anger than their children do when rules are broken
by the kids, this is an indication that the parents are likely
assuming a "victim" stance. By this I mean these parents
feel hopeless and powerless in the face of the children's
misbehaviors and aren't able to successfully issue and
enforce tough-enough consequences (often because they
don't know what to do).

These parents are not effectively remaining In Charge of their children, and their feelings of powerlessness and victimization are the source of their anger. This is one way that parents themselves can hit the Unset button—by somewhat voluntarily giving up their authority over their children.

It's also important for the benefit of rule-breaking children for them to personally feel the anger of the situation. Being angry that actions bring undesirable consequences is a big part of what teaches people to make better choices the next time. Children, however, often thwart this process by blaming their situation on someone else—usually a parent. They fail to fully associate their difficulties with their own decisions and actions. (Some adults also habitually fail to take personal responsibility for their own calamitous choices.) Parents need to strive to help children take responsibility for their own actions. Giving fair and reasonable fitting consequences for undesirable behavior is essential in the process.

Besides accepting powerlessness, there are other ways for parents to hit the Unset button, one of which is to willingly allow or encourage children to make decisions that really should be parental ones. The following questions are extreme and very obvious examples of this:

- "Do you want to play at the park today or go to school?"
- "Would you prefer to eat your dinner or fill up on candy?"
- "Would you like to go to your dental appointment or not?"

Children need their parents to be In Charge and to protect them from their own lack of good judgment in such obviously inappropriate decision-making situations such as these. Thankfully, most parents are In Charge in this kind of way most of the time. However, some parents let children make decisions that are less inappropriate than these but still have the children being overly In Charge.

Parents differ greatly in what they allow children to decide at any given age. Even one parent can differ greatly between children, given their differences. Other than the legal limits to the range of "acceptable" decisions for children of various ages—which limits vary from one jurisdiction to another—there is no definitive authority to give parents precise, mandatory standards. It's a never-ending challenge for parents to guard against both over-allowing and under-allowing children's decisions.

Speaking of decisions, some parenting advisors recommend fabricating decision events for children on a regular basis so as to provide lots of decision-making experience. This practice is also meant to kind of trick the children into thinking they have the lion's share of control over their own lives. With this approach parents are to continually ask young children such things as:

- "Do you want to wear your jacket, your sweater, or just your shirt?"
- "Do you want to drink milk, juice, or water?"

After many such small choices the child makes throughout the day, whenever an unwanted parental decision is about to befall a child, the parent is to announce the intention to take a *turn* at making a decision for the child. For example, the parent might say, "You made all the other decisions today, and now it's my turn to decide. It's bedtime." It seems to me that this method of interaction is designed to deceive and trick the child into compliance with the bigger issues.

In reality, all decisions are not equal. Young children really only have control over the little decisions, and any child with functional brain cells knows it. I'm sure that children can easily discern when decision-making is contrived, and I would imagine they are quite capable of feeling manipulated by such. They likely resent this kind of dishonesty and lose trust in the parent.

Instead of constantly working hard to think up a myriad of choices for my children, I preferred to *let* them and *help* them do their own thinking (a very important life skill). For instance, I preferred to just put the available beverages on the table. I experienced the following:

- Even one-year olds are able to articulate their choices, without any outside prompting, as in, "Joos! Joos! Joos!"
- Two-year olds can do it with table-pounding flair: "I wan' miwk! ... thump ... I wan' miwk! ... thump ... I wan' miwk! ... thump."
- And three-year olds can even do it politely: "Peaz pass uh chockit miwk. ... *Peaz pass uh chockit miwk!* ... ***Peaz pass uh chockit miwk!*** (Elbowing the child to the right.) ARE YUH DEAF? *I SAID PASS UH CHOCKIT MIWK!* ... Oh. ... Elbowing the child to the left.) Pass uh chockit miwk, peaz."

Such decision making comes naturally to children who are raised in nurturing environments. It doesn't need to be taught to them in an artificial, contrived way.

Oh, and children who are given the choice of wearing a jacket, a sweater, or just a shirt will almost always choose just a shirt, even in a blizzard. It's parentally foolish, therefore, to offer such choices in anything remotely like a blizzard or any other adverse condition in which the parent would overrule the child's decision, proving it wasn't really the child's to make after all. In this situation it's better for the parent to simply tell the child to take his coat instead of faking a decision event for the child.

But if parents really would let their children go places without adequate outerwear, they're still much better off not even mentioning the decision options in the first place. Here's why. If the parent offered the selection of choices to the child and then let the child make a bad choice, the child could easily and legitimately come back at the parent with, "Why didn't you make me bring my coat when I didn't want to? Now I'm cold." This would be the child's attempt to place the responsibility for the bad choice on the parent.

If, however, the child was allowed to make an unassisted independent decision to not bring a coat, and then he belatedly realized he was cold, the parent could then legitimately say: "Oh, you didn't think to bring your jacket? I'm sorry. Hopefully you'll think of it next time. I have an extra sweater you can put on. Just roll up the sleeves and you'll be okay."

But in situations where it really doesn't matter what the child chooses to wear, there's still no percentage in formally presenting the decision options to the child. Remember, the main purpose of these falsified decision events is to con the children. The children are allowed to make numerous small decisions throughout the day, and then when a big, important one comes along, the parent claims "a turn" at deciding.

I've never watched parents use this technique on their children, but my guess is that post-toddlers can easily figure out they're being conned by it. I think parents who would choose to con their children in this way in order to hopefully avoid them flipping out over the pronouncement of bedtime, for example, are parents who fear dealing with their children. Why do these parents fear their children? It's undoubtedly because they are not consistently In Charge of their children.

It never seemed like a good thing to me to try to fool my children. I never wanted them accusing me of lying to them. (A few times they accused me anyway, but I was able to defend my perspective in good conscience.) One example of my insistence on the truth for my children was with their immunizations. I remember how nurses, in preparation for giving immunizations to my infants, often told them something ridiculous like, "This won't hurt a bit."

I would always correct the lie. I always warned my infants empathetically, "Owie" just before the nurse gave them their shots. I did this for all of my babies, not just the last eight. They all cried very little or not at all from their immunization shots, even when they were just a month or two old.

Many parents (including myself many years ago) unknowingly hit the Unset button by using a weak tone of voice in dealing with their children. One example of this would be using a high-pitched whining voice when asking children questions like the following one, "Why, why, why won't you put your toys away when I ask?" Another weak-voiced Unset trigger for adults is begging or pleading with children as in, "Please, please, please stop teasing your brother."

If you ever detect yourself using such a walk-all-over-me tone of voice with a child, you would do well to make an immediate readjustment and get back in In Charge mode tout de suite. In order to repair the damage of a whiny communication to a child, as soon as you notice yourself whining, you could self-interrupt with something entertaining like: "Oh, silly me. I know why you won't put your toys away when I ask—because you think I'm your slave and I'm going to do it for you. Heh, heh, heh—I'm not! But I will help you up so you can get it done before lunch, and then you'll get to have a friend over this afternoon if you want to."

Or as soon as you notice yourself begging your child, you could insert a silly "threat" of something your child enjoys (my kids loved being tickled) combined with something they wouldn't like. You could issue these "threats" also in a begging voice, "Because if you don't stop teasing your brother, I might have to tickle you and put you down for a nap." At best, if you self-correct quickly in these ways, your weak moments might not even be detected or might be perceived as on-purpose playfulness. At worst, you will have only brief Unset moments.

There are times when it's appropriate and possibly even crucial, despite the effort and trouble it takes, to take away *all* privileges from a child—such as when the child is on strike or in a state of mutiny. When a child has declared such an In Charge War, the parent might need to swiftly withdraw *all* privileges until child cooperation is restored and the parent is back In Charge. I've had to do this a few times with a few out-of-control mutinous teens.

Some child-rearing advisors recommend that parents take away children's every privilege as a consequence for their each and every misbehavior (whether major or minor). This is overkill. In my experience, for most infractions other than open mutiny, this type of total privilege revoking would be absolutely unnecessary and completely inadvisable. I think children would feel abused if they lost all privileges for committing minor offenses. Besides, taking away every privilege for every offense would be such hard work for the parents, even if they only had one misbehaving child. Children in this country typically have tons of privileges, regardless of their economic status.

For example, children often have the privilege of having a bedroom door. I have been known to take that privilege away from a mutinous teenager or two...or three. However, it doesn't make sense to remove a bedroom door and dozens of other privileges if withholding a fun outing, a treat, a favorite toy, a video game, or a cell phone by itself would have an equal or even better effect. I would rather match a child's loss of privileges in *some* way to the offense, to the child's current attachment to things, or even to some arbitrary thing such as my mood than to automatically take away *every* privilege *every* time.

Here's an example of a particular privilege withdrawal that worked with a particular child. One of my kids was so motivated to earn money that he was employed nonstop from the age of eleven on (starting with a paper route). A few times, around the age of fifteen, he acted like he was so grown up and independent that he didn't have to put up with any kind of parental interference in his personal choices. Of course he actually *did* have to put up with some parental influence because he was living in my home and I was In Charge.

Whenever this son left me no other option and I needed to enforce his compliance, all I had to do was inform him that I would take away his privilege of having a job. Of course he declared that I did not have the right to do that, and I assured him that I did and that I would do it if he didn't comply. It always worked to gain his compliance, because it was what motivated him.

As a discipline technique, I don't like requiring children to somehow earn their confiscated items back. That would be like rubbing salt in the teaching wound by dishing out an extra, unrelated consequence. When the time is up on the privilege confiscation, the consequence should be over.

I wouldn't want a child angrily doing a chore, say washing dishes, so she can get her video game back. I'd rather that she cooperatively washes dishes if and when it's her assigned responsibility or if and when she cheerfully volunteers as a contributing member of the family. The child's emotional growth in response to fair discipline is one important consideration here, but the longevity of the dishes in her angry hands is another. Both of these have improved chances if the child does not suffer added-on anger stemming from added-on consequences or unrelated consequences.

I'm generally against the practice of children being required to articulate back to their parents what offenses were committed. The purpose of this technique, supposedly, is that the parents can then be sure that the children fully understand exactly what they did wrong. Whenever I've observed parents using this technique, however, it seems to malfunction.

In my observation, tell-me-what-you-did-wrong parents tend to be over-controlling and irate and they rant and rave at their children for awhile before demanding that the children name their offending behaviors. I think by the time these children get to the point of articulating their offenses, they must have them memorized word for word, including the why-they're-offensive part. Naming offenses to parents at that point only proves children can memorize and pay attention when on the "hot seat." It does not prove the children understand, care, or agree with the parents about the behaviors.

This particular "hot seat" technique, in fact, does not *encourage* children to understand, care, or agree with parents. I believe it does the exact opposite because parents often do this technique in at least a slightly patronizing or condescending way, and "hot-seating" people in general is usually at least somewhat disrespectful. This method then predisposes children to respond disrespectfully to the disrespect from their parents.

A number of times in the past, I witnessed an even more thorough process than this tell-me-what-you-did-wrong kind of interrogation of children. Whenever a friend of mine had chastised one of his children about some misbehavior he then posed to the child the stern, intimidating question, "What do I want to hear from you?" I agonized with his children during their careful mental searches to find the perfect answers for their father. They came up with some remarkable guesses as to what their dad wanted to hear from them, including what they'd done wrong, why it was wrong, that they wouldn't do it again, and an apology.

I thought this process was not very beneficial to the children, except perhaps to teach them to think under pressure. I suppose it might have been helpful training specifically for dealing with future "hot-seating" bosses, but assertiveness training would, in my opinion, have been more appropriate.

When people are angry with me, I prefer they tell me straight out what they're upset about and why, and how they would like me to change things, without demanding that I reiterate the information back to them or that I offer an apology. I prefer to reiterate and apologize at my discretion, not on demand. I believe this straight forward and respectful communication approach as opposed to any interrogation technique is more likely to help children develop a healthy sense of social responsibility, with less resentment towards their parents.

The only form of this what-do-I-want-to-hear-from-you technique that I think might possibly be necessary for certain children on occasion would be a much more respectful version. Sometime after the initial discussion about the offense, the parents could have a casual conversation with the child in order to get his or her feelings and thinking on the situation, without putting any you-must-understand-this kind of pressure on the child. Then, if during the conversation the parents discover a lack of understanding of the issue on the child's part, they might want to further try to enlighten the child in a respectful way.

One effective and respectful way for parents to do this is to use "I" statements about how they feel. These should be well received by the child if the parents have just listened respectfully to how the child feels. But even for parents' initial dealings with children about misbehaviors, it is highly beneficial to use the "I" Statement Method, which greatly reduces the accusatory feel of the events and the typical defensive reactions of the children. Parents can make "I" statements that indicate what the offense was, why it was offensive, and what is wanted from the children. This can even work well when no child in the family will divulge which one of them is the culprit of a particular crime—as long as only communication (and not the issuing of a consequence) is the parental goal.

In such a scenario, a parent can gather all of the suspects and make "I" statements to the whole group, such as:

- "Since no one will admit spilling shampoo in my bathroom, I just want to say to all of you that I'm annoyed that

    (a) Somebody was messing around with my stuff.
    (b) The mess wasn't cleaned up by the offender.
    (c) I wasn't warned about the mess, and I walked in it and tracked it across my bedroom rug.
    (d) This "investigation" took thirty minutes of my time that I didn't have to spare right now."

The parent in this group approach can then issue prescriptive "I" statements that can let the gathered children know what amends are desired. This tends to extinguish any fears of unknown consequences; thus, encouraging—

though not ensuring—a confession and maybe even an apology from the guilty party. Likewise, an option of continued anonymity encourages at least the making of amends.

This parent's prescriptive "I" statements could include any of the following:

- If anyone would like to take this dry cloth and this wet cloth (which I will leave on the counter) and clean up the shampoo mess, I would appreciate that.
- If anyone would like to do me a favor to compensate for my loss of time—say, for instance, vacuum and dust my bedroom while I'm at my meeting this afternoon—that would also be appreciated.
- If anyone would like to apologize, anonymously or otherwise, that would also be great. There is a notepad and pen by my pillow in case anyone would like to do it in writing.
- And—one last thing—if everyone stays out of my stuff, I would really, really like that.

I'm not a fan of enforced apologies. I don't like requiring or demanding apologies from children by the time they're a certain age. I do, however, teach them apology basics over a number of years. The first part of this process is to show children how apologizing should be done, by modeling the behavior to them. I tried to set a good example for my children by easily apologizing to them (from their birth on) whenever I made mistakes or committed everyday inadvertent offenses that affected them—such as not giving them their bottles as fast as they wanted, bumping into them accidentally, or mistakenly calling them by a sibling's name. I tried to normalize apologizing as an everyday part of life, as it should be.

The second part of teaching apology basics is to model for children how they should apologize to others for their mistakes or inappropriate behaviors. This needs to be done for kids from the toddler stage up to the age of three or four, or maybe five—at which time they should be starting to handle their own apologies, without the parent having to be a constant model.

I did this apology modeling for my very young children by apologizing to other people on their behalf whenever warranted. Within hearing of my child, to an adult I might have said, "I'm sorry my little boy bumped into you." To another child I maybe said, "I'm sorry my little girl knocked over your castle." I didn't have or display any attitude that my as-yet untrained child should be the one making the apology, and I didn't tell or ask my child to apologize. However, I might have asked her to help fix the castle if the other child wanted the help.

After a child had had maybe three to five years of such modeling, I moved to the third level of apology basics—consequence-based instruction. For instance, whenever I felt a child was old enough and should be apologizing to me for something—but wasn't—I'd prompt with, "I feel you owe me an apology." The child then made the decision to apologize or not. If the child chose not to apologize to me, and I was honestly still even mildly upset awhile later when he or she asked for my help with something nonessential, I would consider honestly declining.

I might say the following "I" statement to the child, "Well, right now I'm still upset about what you did and that you haven't apologized, so I don't exactly feel like helping you with that." Mentioning the child's lack of an apology reinforced the concept that the child could fix the problem. I never stated that I *wouldn't* help the child—only that I didn't *feel* like it. This emphasized how my child's behavior affected me emotionally.

After my verbal response to the child's request I simply neglected to go about helping the child as I normally would have done. Depending on the particular child's level of resistance to apologizing, this may or may not have prompted an apology. If not, then the child had the opportunity to learn from the natural consequence of missing out on my help. If so, and if I was able to have a respectful conversation with my child about the problematic behavior, I might have changed my mind about not helping.

At some point in children's exposure to these respectful teaching methods, a parent hopes they learn to apologize genuinely, voluntarily, and primarily without prompting. For many children this happens around about the age of four or five. Teaching apology basics isn't really a whole lot more difficult than teaching children to consistently and independently say please and thank you—which can usually be accomplished by a child's fourth year or earlier.

In order for children to become self-prompting, usually the parent has to first consciously *stop* doing the prompting. It's the same thing whether it's apologizing, saying please and thank you, or doing chores. You can teach kids, for instance, how to do the dishes. And you can make them do them *right now*. But you can't teach them how to make themselves do them when they don't want to and you're not around—unless you first back off and stop telling them to do the chore or at least delay telling them as much as you can tolerate. This gives them some practice in telling themselves, resisting themselves, arguing with themselves, overruling themselves, and so on.

This kind of backing off was the method that once produced a twelve-year-old floor "commander" in my home. He didn't let anyone put anything where it didn't belong, and he swept the floors three times a day without prompting. Of course, teaching children to do chores and backing off from the prompting isn't usually all that's needed to produce such self prompters.

Such results most often take additional tactics, such as saying no to requested outings (either *because* the chores aren't done or *until* the chores *are* done). And even then, some children don't become big-time self prompters until well after they leave home. (These are the ones who will surprise you the most when they thank you years later for teaching them how to work.)

Getting children to habitually say please after they've been adequately taught also usually requires at least some consequence-based actions. What I found to work was simply *not* responding to please-less requests. As if I hadn't heard the requests, I just didn't respond. (At least the first time I did this to each particular child, however, I would look big-eyed in response to maybe the third repetition of the request, by way of a hint that the issue was not sudden deafness.) This method helps even two- and three-year olds quickly form habits of saying please. I never came up with a good consequence for my children's occasional neglect to thank me when they should have. But I might offer them a slightly embarrassing reminder by cheerfully and loudly saying, "You're welcome." That almost always brought out the belated thank you (and usually a chuckle).

It's important for parents to add consequence-based reinforcement to their manners teaching if and when indicated. Parents who don't give consequences to their children for impoliteness can easily end up with disliked seven- and eight-year olds, if not older disliked children. Adults and children who don't follow the social norms for politeness are perceived as disrespectful. People who are perceived as disrespectful are generally not liked.

Let me make a few more points about children and apologies. Seemingly due to personality traits, some kids are highly resistant to apologizing. Even with many years of basic apology modeling, parental backing off from prompting, and the issuing of natural lack-of-apology-related consequences, some children are still apology challenged. I don't see any benefits in going the final (or only) step that some parents take—that of *ordering* children to apologize.

I didn't personally happen to *be* an apology-resistant child. However, I was stubbornly self-nurturing. As a small child I was ordered to apologize a few times when I truly believed I was not guilty of anything. I did apologize because it was in my best interest to do so, but the apologies were not genuine. I was determined to not *feel* sorry even though I had *said* I was sorry. This is the exact opposite of what is likely the intentioned, hoped-for effect of enforced apologies. Personally, I would rather my children give me genuine apologies or none.

Not demanding apologies from children helps in the process of disciplining. Without an enforced, fake apology, it's easier to see that children aren't really sorry for their behavior if such is the case. And then it's possible to include the child's lack of remorse when considering a consequence.

For instance, a parent might say: "I'm not giving you an ice cream cone because you knocked your brother's into the dirt on purpose. I'm also going to have you stay by yourself in your room for awhile because you don't seem to be the least bit sorry for your offensive behavior. When you're ready, I'd like to talk to you about what happened and why you don't seem to be sorry for what you did. Okay?"

This approach would give the parent an excellent opportunity to talk respectfully with the child about appropriate responses to anger (or whatever else had initiated the ice-cream-cone incident) and about appropriate expressions of sorrow for relationship offenses. It would also give the child time to analyze the whole event and perhaps come to the conclusion that an apology is, after all, the right action to take.

Chapter Nine Summary: Other Consequences and Parenting Techniques

- Parents would do well to develop useful repertoires of versatile neutral statements that they can use as substitutes for confrontational direct orders.

- Besides making consequences fit the offenses of your children, it also helps to make each consequence fit the offender. In other words, if you're going to take away a privilege from a child, make sure it's a privilege that the child cares about losing.

- It helps a whole lot when dishing out consequences to have them thought up ahead of time.

- Rule-breaking children should be the ones to feel the anger, not the parents.

- Parents can hit the Unset button by somewhat voluntarily giving up authority over their children, by allowing or encouraging children to make decisions that really should be parental ones, and by using a weak tone of voice (whining or begging).

- Some parenting advisors recommend fabricating decision events for children. I prefer to *let* them and *help* them do their own thinking (a very important life skill).

- Some child-rearing advisors recommend that parents take away children's every privilege as a consequence for their each and every misbehavior (whether major or minor). This is overkill.

155

- I'm generally against the practice of children being required to articulate back to their parents what offenses were committed.

- When parents deal with children about their misbehaviors, it is highly beneficial to use the "I" Statement Method (which greatly reduces the accusatory feel and the typical defensive reaction of the child).

- I'm not a fan of enforced apologies. Rather than requiring or demanding apologies from children by the time they're a certain age, I prefer to teach them apology basics over a number of years.

Chapter Ten: Respect

Teaching children to be respectful human beings is a multifaceted process. They need to learn to respect social rules. They need to learn to show basic respect to everyone, including to those in authority over them, to those they are in authority over, to people who are different than them, and to those who are disrespectful to them (while not accepting the disrespect). Respect needs to be taught to children in a number of ways: by the parent and others modeling respectful behavior; through the giving of explicit instructions and information about social rules; and by giving consequences for disrespectful behavior.

Teaching respectful behavior to children is a very important part of raising them. Respectful behavior is important in many aspects of life, including in establishing functional lasting relationships, avoiding unnecessary conflict, acquiring what is needed and wanted, functioning well in a career or business, and being a likeable human being.

Parents need to be In Charge of their children in a respectful way while simultaneously not accepting disrespect from them. To accomplish this, it is helpful to have the attitude that each person in the family is equally important and that everyone's needs are equally important. Of course, children's urgent needs often take precedence or have higher priority over parents' needs, but that is not the same thing as having more importance.

This concept of equal importance might seem to be so basic that it doesn't even need mentioning; however, families don't always function in such an egalitarian manner. Some families assign Dad and/or Mom more importance than the children. Some family members assign themselves more importance than everyone else. And some families are extremely child-focused, child-centered, or child-important, to the detriment of the parents.

Whenever there is an imbalance in the importance of people in a family, there automatically follows an imbalance of respect. For many decades in our society, in general, parenting advisors, child development professionals, and social commentators have implicitly assigned less importance to mothers than to fathers and children. Generally, this translates into lower status and less respect for mothers. Just one way this has often played out in everyday living is in an unequal and heavier-than-fair share of the family work load expected to be done by mothers, and a lighter-than-fair share by the fathers and children.

People who are conditioned to accepting disrespect and to being treated as less important than others are sometimes not consciously aware of their plight. If they don't recognize they are being disrespected and devalued, they make no effort to stand up to the disrespectful treatment. But even when people face these same issues with full awareness, they can find it difficult or impossible (and in some cases highly unsafe) to stand up to the disrespect. Some mothers are in this category in dealing with their husbands and their children, especially the preteens and teens.

Mothers who have difficulty standing up to the disrespect of their children often have partners who openly fault them for this. Some of these same partners actually contribute in various ways to the problem—sometimes as negative role models for the disrespectful children. These types of family dynamics are difficult to heal but not always impossible—especially with outside help. Families that are dealing with importance and respect imbalances such as these could potentially benefit from the help of a wise counselor.

It can be very challenging to tackle such heavy-duty family issues. (When it doesn't feel physically safe to openly confront issues, we shouldn't do it without proper support and backup). Otherwise, though, for our own peace of mind, we need to try every reasonable thing to solve issues with our children, to keep giving them another chance to get it right, and to keep doing the best we can. Despite the challenges involved, parents need to guard against viewing themselves as less important than their children (and accepting disrespect from them) and against treating their children as less important than themselves (and being disrespectful to them).

It's very important that children don't get away with the blatant disrespect of physically or verbally attacking their parents or attempting to. Hitting, kicking, biting, pinching, spitting, intimidating, name-calling, and such are very dramatic Unset actions that children often try out. If they don't receive adequate consequences for these behaviors, they may then continue to use them.

Of course, it isn't possible to stop every attempt at these from every child every time because kids have more time to watch for opportune moments than parents have to watch for sneak attacks. But when a child *is* able to "land one," the parent must not allow it or accept it. In other words, the parent must firmly convey that such will not be tolerated and then issue a reasonable consequence. Without doing that the parent is allowing the disrespect, and the child will most likely continue it as a very convenient, quick, easy, and forceful Unset technique.

Every one of my babies (at about the age of six months old) started to go through a stage of randomly, without warning, smacking me in the face or head when being held by me. It didn't happen very often—maybe once every week or two. I have no idea why my babies hit me like this, except I'm guessing the first time for each was possibly accidental. Perhaps their large-motor skills at that age, being still rather new, were somewhat tricky to use. Subsequent episodes may have partially stemmed from their desires to liven things up. Who's to say! But this problem was the same with my post-empathy babies as it was for all of my pre-empathy ones.

I'm pretty sure I wasn't in any way provoking my babies' attacks on me, and they were too young at the time to be into hidden aggression. They never observed older children or anyone else hitting me, so they weren't copying that kind of example. However, all but the first two babies likely observed siblings hitting other siblings on a fairly regular basis. (My childhood had been happily free of physical fighting with my three siblings, so I was deeply disappointed that my children refused to follow this behavior pattern.)

Initially with each smacking baby I responded to their attacks verbally, with a yelp or some equivalent, then firmly grasped the offending baby hand and equally firmly said something to the effect that it was not okay to hit me (the No Hit-Message Method). My babies always seemed to be studying my reactions to their smacks. And I studied their studying of my reactions.

They seemed smart enough to *appear* dumb. In other words, they appeared intent on *appearing* free of malicious intent. Their facial expressions said: "I'm just an innocent baby;" "Don't look at *me*—my arm has a mind of its own!" But behind the masks of innocence there always seemed to be other things going on. Although they never actually smirked, they often had the post-smack essence of smirks. I could sense the baby-brain wheels turning out thoughts like: "Wow! Such a great reaction for such a small effort! That was kind of fun. I'll have to try that again sometime when I'm bored.

With each infant, I tried to get the behavior to stop by using the No-Hit Message Method, usually for a couple of months or so. With my last child I tried this method for much longer—maybe six months. I thought perhaps I just hadn't tried long enough with my earlier children for the method to correct the problem.

I never tried putting my babies in their cribs as a form of consequence or Time-out for this smacking behavior. Most of the smacks they gave me didn't occur during fun together time, so putting them in their cribs wouldn't have seemed like an actual consequence. Most of the smacks occurred when we were busy going somewhere or doing something, and it wouldn't have always been convenient or possible to do a Time-out. My babies were also probably too young to logically connect a crib Time-out with the smack offense. With each baby, I eventually gave up on the No-Hit Message Method because it didn't stop the behavior. (They were essentially receiving no consequences, so they continued with the behavior.)

Through the years I asked a number of other mothers what worked for them to stop this kind of infant-to-parent violence, but (astonishingly) none of them had ever heard of such a parenting problem. Go figure—all thirteen of my children versus none of theirs. (Another thing I've always puzzled over is why none of my children ever sucked their thumbs. What causes thumb sucking?)

With each child, I eventually decided I had to give up on the No-Hit Message Method and convert to the Reciprocal Method. Usually only once or twice each, when the babies smacked me I returned the smacks. My smacks to the babies were very carefully placed so as to not cause any harmful or lasting effects; were soft enough to not leave any marks of any kind; were just hard enough to get the baby's attention and teach that it is unpleasant to be hit; and they were usually a little or a lot less forceful than the babies' smacks to me. I always added firm and loving verbal instruction to the physical teaching by saying things like: "Don't hit me. It hurts. This is what it feels like. Owie." If the baby cried in response to the return smack, I gave empathy. The Reciprocal Method was always a very quick and effective way of ending the problem.

I have never had the problem of my toddlers and older children hitting me because they all learned not to at a younger age. So I'm not sure if toddlers and older children who've been getting away with hitting a parent will generally stop the behavior, short of the parent using the Reciprocal Method. But I would hope so.

The important thing, however, is that the child needs to consistently receive an unpleasant (but fair) consequence for hitting the parent. Children (as opposed to babies) are capable of responding well to many different consequences, such as Groundings and the loss of privileges that are connected logically to the offense. For instance, to a toddler or older child, a parent could communicate the following: "I've told you it's not okay to hit me *even if* you're mad about not getting your way. Because you hit me when I wouldn't take you to the store, you are now not going to get any fun privileges for the rest of the day, and I'm cancelling our swimming trip for Saturday. I'm not going to reward you when you are disrespectful to me. Hitting me is a deal breaker."

One thing that I found helpful in educating even very young babies to be respectful in general was to teach them that there are public places where it is expected of them to be quiet. Now, I know there are *plenty* of parents who don't believe *their* adorable children should ever have to be quiet in public places. I *know* this because countless certifiably adorable children in swimming pools over the years have emitted award-quality extreme-volume impressively-lengthy perfectly-placed screeches directly into one of my unsuspecting ear canals. This was done while the spectator parent smiled and waved proudly and approvingly as if to say:

"Wonderful screeching, son! You're obviously having oodles of fun! And that must obviously mean that I'm a terrific parent!"

Also, I've often gone out to eat (and to get a break from my own children) only to have to tolerate other people's noisy, rambunctious, and un-shushed children in the restaurant. There are plenty of parents who claim to want their children to be well-behaved in public but who also proclaim (perhaps because of their own lack of success) that young children are incapable of such. Many of those parents have asked me in awe, "How do you get your kids to sit quietly in public like that?"

Partly I did it by starting when each child first began to make talking noises in public—about three or four months old. I taught them to be reasonably quiet in public simply by touching one finger to their lips and one to mine, smiling, shaking my head, and almost inaudibly saying, "Shhh." I did this whenever they were even slightly louder than what was desirable for the situation. In a library or similar place I probably did it to any of my infants who made any talking noise at all. I did not expect people in public to adjust to my naturally noisy children as most parents seem to do these days. I expected my three-month-old babies to learn when to be quiet. And they did—easily.

Of course, if these little babies in public needed something that could potentially induce them to cry, I would take care of their need as soon as I recognized it. I wouldn't expect them to be quiet if they had to communicate a need to me.

By the time my children were toddlers, they were already very able, with very little direction, to modify their volume as appropriate to each public circumstance. However, they did need some ongoing instructions and direction as they matured. When my children were toddlers and older, besides pleasantly shushing them, I would briefly and

163

factually explain the need for quiet and respectful behavior in each situation. I might say, "Other people are trying to hear the movie, so you need to be quiet." Or I might simply give a neutral statement such as, "Children in stores are expected to be reasonably quiet."

I've found that toddlers are very capable of and intrigued with learning to whisper. I mean a true whisper, with no sound at all coming from the voice box. I've met a few adults, however, who either can't or won't do a genuine whisper, even to avoid disturbing others. This has often puzzled, irritated, and—whenever it was one of my last two spouses—embarrassed me. It puzzled me because by that time I already knew for a fact that even toddlers can and do learn to whisper. All of my children were taught early on that whispering was sometimes an expected behavior in public.

I also taught my children (starting as soon as they were old enough to scream at play) that their screaming should not be used for playing, either in public or at home. My theory is that screaming should be used only for emergencies, as a signal that help is needed. (Yelling is okay during play, though.) Emergency-only screaming is important for children to learn so that their caretakers and others will actually come running when help is needed, instead of thinking the kids are just playing. But it's also important in showing respect for others people's eardrums.

I tried to teach my children other respectful behaviors as well. I taught them that closing their mouths when eating is respectful of people like me who have absolutely no ability to tolerate lip-smacking, food crunching, gum popping and snapping, and other obnoxious nourishment-related noises. (This issue of mine is similar in kind and in intensity to other people's inability to tolerate fingernails scraping on blackboards.) My children were also taught not to pat-pat-pat-pat-pat me or other people when seeking attention. (This, of course, is another one of my "pat" peeves.)

In the first decade or so of my parenting, I endured occasional frustration with the socially average unruliness of my children during family outings. Even though my kids didn't misbehave worse than most other people's, there were more of them. So it was still pretty exasperating at times.

That brings up a point I want to make about patience. It's funny to me how people have so often assumed that because I have a ton of children, I have a ton of patience. Their assumption is that patience in childrearing is multiplication-based. (Four times the children automatically equals four times the patience.) Of course, there is some increase in patience that is connected to more experience and such, but that's more like addition—of fractions—than multiplication.

The reality is that patience in parenting is division-based. Each parent has x amount of patience (some more than others). That finite amount of patience is shared or divided by the number of children involved. In other words, if I have two children, I sometimes let either or both of them use up all or most of my patience before I put the breaks on their inappropriate behavior. If I have ten children, they as a group occasionally get to use up whatever patience I possess before I put a stop to their shenanigans.

Anyway, in that first decade or two of my parenting, as the number of my children grew, so did the level of my exasperation. My patience was being spread thinner and thinner, you might say, with less and less available per child than before. I was seeking out new and improved ways of getting consistent cooperation from my children. I was constantly trying to think up new ways to thwart any unacceptable behavior they were trying to think up. One successful way was my first husband's idea, which I've already mentioned—seating and timing the kids on chairs for their public unruliness.

Another method I came up with was also consistently successful. When my children became too rowdy in public or in my vehicle, I matter-of-factly brought out pen and paper and started quietly recording demerits and bonus points per person. The tallying of these points later helped determine the amount of ice cream or whatever each child would be receiving after the event. All I had to do during the outing was relax, pay detached attention to the children's behavior, and make check marks in various columns. It usually only took a minute or two until one of them noticed my tallying and everyone settled down appropriately.

I remember another thing I came up with about the same time I started counting Ice Cream Points. It may not have helped improve my children's behavior any, but it definitely helped me by validating my experience.

After a particularly difficult drive home from the beach one day with my unappreciative, squabbling children, I created a sign for the back of my fifteen-passenger van. It read:

CAUTION!

This van may be filled with children ...
And the driver may be in a foul mood!

The sign endured through six years of other motorists laughing and counting kids through tinted windows and the occasional pump jockey cautiously enquiring about my mood before filling my tank. My teens at the time never seemed to appreciate the joke much, and they occasionally complained, "Someone's counting us again. Duck everybody!" So the sign's eventual disappearance wasn't a total mystery. Some year in the future, possibly at a family reunion, I expect to hear my suspicions of teenage sign sabotage confirmed.

My success in teaching my children to behave respectfully depended to a high degree on the level of expectations I held for them. I didn't realize this, however, until about eight years into my parenting career. That's when a wise friend, Jim Hillyer, shared a profound bit of child-rearing philosophy with me. He said, "Children will always perform just a little under our expectations of them."

That really got me thinking and analyzing my existing expectations for my children. I decided that I needed to increase my expectations—considerably. So I did. And true to the axiom, my children's performance improved—considerably—to the point that numerous people in my community gushed at how well my kids behaved in public. My children, like most people's, were much less likely to behave properly at home, of course, as parents everywhere can attest. But in general, in all categories where I increased my expectations, my children's performance improved.

Of course, it is possible for parents to have the opposite problem to the one I generally had. It's possible for parents to hold out such high expectations for their children that none could possibly come close to measuring up. I've heard of such situations where parents actually need to lighten up on their kids. But that was *definitely* not me—nope!

Teaching children to behave respectfully is a whole lot easier for parents if they themselves have learned to show basic respect to everyone. On the other hand, parents who interact disrespectfully with others, and especially with their own children, have a much more difficult time teaching respectful behavior. Children seem to easily assimilate modeled disrespectful behavior patterns into their own behavioral repertoires.

Some common parent-to-child disrespect patterns that kids copy easily include when parents fail to apologize to their children at appropriate times; direct belittling, name-calling, or sarcasm at their children; assign blame to their children unnecessarily; and blame their children for their own mistakes. One example of a parent inappropriately blaming children is the accusatory statement, "You kids made me miss my left turn." A better approach would be to complain, "I missed my left turn when you guys were fighting in the backseat." (This is another example of the difference between "You" statements and "I" statements.) If parents want to teach respectful behavior to children, they need to make every effort to model it, including correcting any patterns of disrespect in their own behavior.

Chapter Ten Summary: Respect

- Teaching children to be respectful is a multifaceted process that can be done through explicit instructions, parental modeling of respectful behavior, and giving consequences for disrespectful behavior.

- Parents need to be In Charge of their children in a respectful way while simultaneously not accepting disrespect from them. Each person in the family—and each person's needs—are equally important.

- Children should not get away with the blatant disrespect of physically or verbally attacking their parents or even attempting to. These are very dramatic Unset actions that require adequate consequences.

- It's possible to start teaching even very young babies to be generally respectful.

  o I started when each child first began to make talking noises in public—about three or four months old. I would touch one finger to their lips and one to mine, smiling, shaking my head, and very quietly saying, "Shhh." I did this whenever they were even slightly louder than what was desirable for the situation.
  o When my children were toddlers and older, I would briefly and factually explain the need for quiet and respectful behavior in each situation.
  o I taught my toddlers how to whisper. I also taught my children that their screaming should not be used for playing. Screaming should only be used for emergencies as a signal that help is needed.
  o I taught my children that closing their mouths when eating is respectful of people who can't tolerate lip-

169

smacking noises. I taught them that patting people while trying to get their attention is a behavior that some people find very annoying.

- The reality is that patience is division-based. One parent has x amount of patience. That amount of patience is shared or divided by the number of children involved.

- One successful method of shutting down my children's rowdy, disrespectful behavior in public or in my vehicle was to matter-of-factly bring out pen and paper and quietly record demerits and bonus points. These points helped determine the amount of ice cream or whatever each child would be receiving after the event.

- Children will always perform just a little under our expectations of them.

- If parents want to teach respectful behavior to children, they need to make every effort to model it, including correcting any patterns of disrespect in their own behavior.

Chapter Eleven: Parental Consistency

You might be surprised (or not) to find out that I think the concept of consistency in parenting is highly overrated. Parents are continually admonished to be consistent in virtually all things parental. You know, no parent can be that consistent. No set of parents taking turns around the clock can be that consistent, even with only one child. And you know what? No kid expects, wants, or needs a parent to be one hundred percent consistent.

If a home-cooked dinner isn't served in the dining room exactly at 6:00 P.M. every evening with everyone in attendance, your family won't fall apart. If bedtimes fluctuate somewhat, oh well. You can get back on track as soon as possible. If you don't always attend exactly equal numbers of events per child, you won't damage them beyond repair.

The occasional times that you waive, don't enforce, or change rules because you're too busy, too tired, too upset, or too distracted can be explained to your children. These situations have a chance to teach them that life isn't always consistent, scheduled, black-and-white, or cut-and-dried. Here are some examples:

- "Ryan, you can finish putting your toys away tonight. Jimmy needs stitches, and I have to take him to the hospital right now. I'll drop you off at Mary's. She's going to take you to preschool today, okay?"

- "Kendra, alright, you can stay up an extra hour if you sleep in a half hour in the morning and get ready for school faster. But that would mean you'd have to get your lunch and clothes ready tonight."

- "Right now I *have* to focus on my project, and I don't have time to deal with your defiance, so you might just get away with it. Or not. Depends."
"On what?"
"Many things. (Including my memory.) But I'll just make a note on my calendar to help me out. And if my calendar goes missing, I'll know who to look for. Ha Ha Ha."

These kinds of inconsistencies don't equate to flushing all of your teachings down the toilet. I think there's such a thing as too much consistency where children aren't given enough opportunities to learn spontaneity and flexibility and to cope with change. That reminds me of a trick my first mother-in-law taught me about babies. She'd had nine children, and I was on my first. She said that if I purposely picked up and moved my sleeping newborn every once in awhile and did not isolate him from the normal household noise, he would learn to sleep through everything. He did! And so did all the rest of my kids.

I also learned other little inconsistency advantages that prevented me from overprotecting and over-sheltering my kids from healthy flexibility. Not that I had much choice in the matter, with having so many children and the inevitable schedule disruptions, but I didn't even try to establish highly rigid schedules and routines with my children. Actually I think ours were only barely rigid...once in awhile.

Because of our family's rather flexible nature, the children learned to easily adapt and adjust when necessary. If, for example, a child occasionally wasn't able to do homework at home during the preferred time right after school— due to a spontaneous family shopping trip or something— she was easily able to adjust and do it in the car or later.

For their various personal reasons, I often allowed my children to chore-switch between siblings. This taught them all the art of negotiation. Also, as much as possible I let my children preselect their own chores for the month, encouraging greater cooperation from them. In order to encourage children's self-prompting, as much as I could put up with it, I allowed the children to decide *when* to do their chores. (But I often denied a requested or expected privilege or outing *until* the chores were done, which usually motivated them wonderfully.) My children also generally learned to manage their own time at quite a young age because I didn't do that for them either any more than I had to. Allowing my children these kinds of flexibilities contributed to the somewhat chaotic, semi-consistent aspects of our lifestyle.

Many of my less-than-rigid and less-than-consistent approaches (that I viewed as beneficial) evolved out of a chat I once had with another mother. At the time I didn't yet have any teenagers, and she was on her fourth or fifth. She had obviously been exasperated with her kids for awhile. That day she informed me, "Teenagers are the most ungrateful people on the face of the earth!" This kind of scared me, actually. I felt like responding with, "Too much information!" But then I've never been much of a head-in-the-sand kind of person, so I went about processing and assessing the info.

I was already raising five future teenagers by that time, and I was planning more. I was more than a bit rattled by the thought of having a horde of ungrateful teens in my future care. I wanted to discover if there was something I could do differently that might make my experience less disappointing or less exasperating than the other mother's. I didn't have a whole lot of information to go on; however, I knew that she was a stay-at-home mom and did a lot for her children, as did most mothers. Somehow I recognized that fact as possibly my biggest clue.

I pondered the problem. I wondered whether or not teens might appreciate *more* if a parent actually did *less*. In other words, would a parent who deliberately did less than average for a teenager get more appreciation than average from the teen? I hypothesized that it might be good for children and teens for the parents to refrain from doing for them what they are actually capable of doing for themselves (other than justifiable exceptions of course). I can't remember exactly how I came up with this bit of reasoning, but it seemed worth checking into.

So I tested out my supposition and learned a lot about doing and not doing for my children. I learned that it was highly beneficial to all of us if I helped my children become capable and willing to do things for themselves. For instance, I found that six-year olds are highly capable of making their own school lunches. Six-year olds can gather cookies, drink boxes, and fruit; make sandwiches; and put it all in bags before they go out the door for school. What they *aren't* particularly competent at is always remembering to take the lunch bags out the door with them. But that's a reality no matter who makes the lunches. My children made their own school lunches from the first grade on, while other kids' moms made their lunches for them, sometimes into junior high.

Within a year or so after the start of my Doing-Less Initiative, I received much more impetus along the same path. In summary: I survived fourteen months of severe sleep deprivation with a severely colicky baby; immediately thereafter began a pre-desired pregnancy; immediately sunk into five months of depression, migraines, and often being bedridden; depended on my children to regularly help with basic household chores; realized they were *capable* of helping regularly with basic household chores; realized I would survive another baby, colicky or not, and climbed out of the depression; realized I should be expecting my *capable* children to help regularly with basic household chores even though I was now functional again; and assigned regular chores to my children from that day to this.

As my children grew in number, age, and capability, they gradually took over most of the household chores, including laundry and cooking. They also helped with occasional cleaning, deep-cleaning, gardening, canning, and freezing garden produce. Because the household chores were being done by children who also attended school and did homework and who often resisted having to do the chores, I believe we lived with less consistency than most families did.

Once in awhile one of the teenagers would complain to me that they did everything and I did nothing. At such times I would bring out my comprehensive ready-made list of my duties, including shopping, budgeting, banking, chauffeuring, shopping, bill paying, gardening, hair cutting, supervising children's chores, shopping, baking bread... I would post this lengthy, full-page list alongside the children's chore lists and not hear any more complaining.

I can't say for sure that my teenagers ended up more grateful than average, but I believe they did. Countless times they and my younger children thanked me profusely for mending a shirt or doing something that would have been taken for granted by teens in some families. In fact, they thanked me *so* profusely it was often embarrassing. I was glad many times that no one outside of the family heard this excessive gratitude; else they might falsely think I rarely did anything for my kids. Well, maybe in the case of mending it wouldn't have been so false.

I think the biggest advantage of Doing Less for my kids, however, was that they benefited greatly from feeling so capable. Many of my children have reported to me that they grew up feeling very confident about their abilities and skills. They developed more skills at a younger age than children in other families typically did. I found in general (if given a chance) children are safely—if not skillfully—able to do most chores at least a year or two ahead of whatever age is recommended by most child-rearing advisors.

For instance, I let my little children attempt to pour their own milk as young as they wanted to, which was obviously always before they were able to (usually at about the age of two). But they always learned fairly quickly—and without wasting too much milk. I found that children's interest in learning things usually matched their readiness for learning them. Here's an example. At the age of three, one of my daughters started this conversation from the back seat of the car:

"Mommy, buy me thome oiyow?"
"Oiyow?" I asked.
"Yeth! Thome kicking oiyow."
"Kicking oiyow?"
"Yeth, tho I can learn to kick!"
"Ooooooh...you mean *cooking oil!*"

I really thought she should learn to talk before she learned to cook, but she kept asking me, so I taught her. Another three-year-old daughter, a couple of decades later, insisted on being taught how to mix our humongous pans of rice pudding and bake them. From three years old on, she also made scrambled eggs and numerous other dishes for the whole family.

The rest of my children (including the boys) all started learning to cook and bake as part of their regular chores at the more typical age of eight or so. But sometimes I would assign even younger children as cook's helpers. I tried to be flexible in teaching skills to my children, according to their preferences, personal timelines, and individual inclinations. Of course, they all had to eventually learn to do the least-favorite chores, whether or not they wanted to. As much as possible, though, I tried *not* to follow a rigid plan of my own.

I loved what all of this did for my children. They all became flexible individuals who were eager and unafraid to learn new skills and who could easily handle normal change. I could wake small, medium, or large children up in the van when we occasionally arrived home late in the evening, and every one of them would simply plod off to bed without crying or whining. If our car didn't start, and we had to stay home instead of going swimming, they would matter-of-factly put the swimsuits and towels away. They'd figure out some other fun thing to do at home while confirming, "We can go swimming next week, right?"

Given today's socially imposed, professionally recommended parental-consistency standards—which can be interpreted as mandatory one hundred percent consistency—I'm sure I could find at least a few advisors and their faithful followers who would consider the deliberate moving about of sleeping babies to be *tantamount* to *child abuse*. Based on my experience, to those people I would attest that moving a sleeping baby does absolutely no harm. And I believe my somewhat inconsistent and variable parenting style did no harm. But not helping a child develop functional levels of flexibility and spontaneity and a healthy tolerance for change is potentially very detrimental in the long term.

Apparently most adults in our society are at least somewhat fearful and dysfunctional (both personally and professionally) when it comes to making changes. In fact, there are multitudes of workshops available for change-challenged adults where they can work on becoming more comfortable with and less fearful of change. Many of my counseling and psychology courses included change workshops precisely because making changes is such a commonly difficult thing for most people. *I*, however, think I could have *taught* the workshops without an ounce of emotional preparation or warning. And likely all of my kids could have. I doubt that any of them will ever have to attend a change workshop.

Now, please don't think that I'm advocating all-over-the-map extreme inconsistency. That would be fairly traumatic for most kids to endure but especially so for those who tend to be very organized by nature. And it would create unnecessary and possibly unmanageable chaos for the parents. This could potentially lead to their emotional instability or even premature parental retirement.

I'm talking about being somewhat flexible, spontaneous, versatile, and variable (especially in the face of unpreventable change) while being stable, reliable, and dependable. Does that make sense? I think the average kinds of inconsistency that typical families face is good preparation for children's eventual entry into the adult world. I think it's more important to feed a child who is hungry than one who is scheduled to eat. I think it's more important to go to sleep when tired than exactly by the clock. And I think it's sad that many parenting advisors have inflicted unnecessary guilt on parents for non-critical inconsistencies.

What's really important about being consistent as parents is that we accomplish it some of the time. No, just kidding. What's really important is that we apply the consistency principle where it really matters the most. And that is in being respectful, loving, and firmly In Charge of our children (which includes meeting their needs to the best of our abilities). It's important to find firm and loving ways to hit the Reset button as soon as possible after we or our children have hit the Unset button.

Chapter Eleven Summary: Parental Consistency

- No parent can be one hundred percent consistent, and no kid expects, wants, or needs a parent to be so. Life isn't always consistent, scheduled, black-and-white, or cut-and-dried. There's such a thing as too much consistency where children aren't given enough opportunities to learn spontaneity and flexibility and to cope with change.

- What's really important about consistency is that we apply it where it really matters—in being respectful, loving, and firmly In Charge of our children.

MegaMom's Wisdom for Tantrums

Chapter Twelve: Application of the Principles for Eliminating and Preventing Tantrums

I have theorized that the cause of Type-Two Temper Tantrums is a combination of the lack of a timely, caring, and empathetic response from the parent to the initial anger, plus some form of the parent not being adequately or consistently In Charge. This theory does not come from personal experience in dealing with and eliminating Type-Two Tantrums in my own children because I didn't have any such experience. My children only ever threw Type-One Tantrums. My theory is based on my study and analyses of a good many publicly displayed Type-Two Tantrums and the parental responses to them, in comparison with what I had always done differently that prevented Type-Two Tantrums in my children.

In all of the Type-Two Temper Tantrum incidents I witnessed, the parents all exhibited similar responses to one another. They all remained intent on calmly ignoring the tantrums, did not offer any empathy for their children's anger, did not try to reason with the children, and assumed a helpless stance, allowing the children to be In Charge. In spite of the tantrums, all of the parents appeared to be carrying on with whatever they'd been doing before the tantrums erupted. They did seem, however, to have in-creased their speed so as to get out of the public place more quickly. They all seemed to be tuning out and ignoring the significance of the tantrums—that observers around them were annoyed, disapproving, and judgmental. Parents either patiently waited for the tantrums to fizzle all on their own, or they nonchalantly got out of the public eye as quickly as possible.

The practice of quickly giving empathy for pre-tantrum anger is just as important in preventing Type-Two Tantrums as Type-Ones. Children who have learned to resort to manipulation when angry are certainly as needing and deserving of empathy for their anger as anyone else is. Even when children are suspected of embellishing or faking their initial anger, there are still two good reasons to give empathy. They are:

1. Since it is impossible to know for *sure* if the suspicion of faked anger is justified, and the children could be experiencing *some* real anger, it's better to be safe than sorry and give them empathy. Even manipulative children cannot argue with or fault the parent for true expressions of empathy, though they may try to ignore it.
2. Even if children are totally faking the initial anger, they still experience the emotion of it on some level. It's true. Acting or faking emotional scenarios in role-plays elicits real emotions in the participants (though somewhat subdued from what the real and normal emotions would be). And when role-players are given empathy in response to their faked anger, they actually respond to it emotionally. If you don't believe me, do some role-playing with another adult. Pretend to be angry and see how you feel when receiving empathy. But be prepared—especially if you've been empathy-starved for any length of time—you could actually shed a few self-nurturing tears in response to the faked situation.

When parents give empathy in response to the anger of their Type-One or Type-Two Tantrum throwers, they should also cease all ignoring behaviors. I repeat: it's not okay to slide back into ignoring behavior after giving empathy. This may be challenging for hardened Type-Two Tantrum parents because they could potentially feel at a loss when giving up their standard tune-out tool of ignoring. Parents in this category may want to seriously prepare by thoroughly thinking through and planning responses ahead of time.

This preparation could include writing down all potential responses to all typical circumstances that lead to the Type-Two Tantrums. Parents could then select the best response for each, keeping in mind the core principles of empathy, respect, and being In Charge. A list of these best possible responses should be kept handy for easy reference until the parents have no more need of it.

So, *how*, you ask (besides giving empathy) should parents of Type-Two Tantrum throwers react to the tantrums until they cease to occur? If at all possible—even before one more tantrum has had a chance to erupt—the first step should be for the parents to try to change the overall relationship dynamics by consistently being In Charge in a firm and loving way.

Depending on the age of the children, the parents may even want to explain to them the impending changes or new rules. For example, the parents might communicate the following: "I'm not always going to be giving you Time-outs for misbehavior anymore. Sometimes I'm going to be thinking up new consequences when you don't do what I tell you. And from now on when you throw a tantrum, it's not going to get you what you want. I've learned some new ways to help you behave more respectfully."

When some child anger does show up, empathy should be given as soon as possible. If there's still the sense that a Type-Two Tantrum is imminent, another layer of empathy should be laid out while the parent tries to think up a way to hit the Reset button or tries to remember what the pre-planned response was. Depending on the child and the circumstance, it might work in the middle of the tantrum buildup to say, "Hold that thought while I go get my list of consequences, will you?"

Many parenting advisors recommend that parents Time-out or constrain their children for the duration of a tantrum, while otherwise ignoring it. This is even recommended for tantrums in public places. I have already made clear my general views on Time-outs and ignoring.

My view on allowing a child to scream in public until voluntarily finished is that it permits the child to show disrespect to others. It's allowing the airwaves shared with other people to be tainted—a similar scenario to allowing someone to contaminate communal air with tobacco smoke. Allowing a child to scream at will in public isn't properly preparing that child for the realities of functioning in school or any other public venue. I also don't see any benefits to leaving the tantrum to continue in a public place if other options are available.

I would recommend immediately removing the child from the public place (if at all possible) while adding more empathy to the situation and telling the child that screaming in a public place is not allowed. While exiting the premises, I would suggest saying matter-of-factly to people along the path, "I apologize for my child's behavior." This would help the parent, the child, and any onlookers correctly view the issue as the child's problem. The child might even subdue the tantrum behavior in order to hear what is being said to the onlookers, who themselves might be less annoyed and judgmental.

If the parent seriously has a need to issue a Time-out for a public Type-Two Tantrum, it could be somewhat removed from the public and supervised in the car, in a stroller, or in the parking lot. If the tantrum was thrown because the child wanted to leave the public place, I would recommend removing the child until calm and then returning when the tantrum was over. I would, however, have a firm and loving conversation with the child before returning, using a lot of "I" statements. I would probably also issue an additional consequence (based on The 2-3X Principle). If the child refused to return to the public place with me, I would consider issuing a more severe additional consequence.

A screaming tantrum in a public place is Unset behavior for its entire duration *even if* the child is restrained. Riding it out where it begins equals leaving the Unset action unchallenged. However, if the child is removed from the public place and screams, say, in the car seat, the parent can give additional empathy and declare that there will be a consequence after the tantrum. The child can be informed, "As soon as you're ready to talk about your anger instead of screaming, I will be happy to be within earshot of you." If it's safe to do so, the parent can then wait a short distance away, outside the car, for the tantrum to subside. If the parent isn't comfortable waiting outside the vehicle, ear plugs could be used inside. This way of dealing with the public tantrum would not be a *total* Reset. But it would at least be a *partial* Reset.

Physically restraining children during tantrums could potentially have some negative impact. I would only recommend using this technique when absolutely necessary for the purpose of the children's safety or for children who are unable to learn from other methods. Using this technique during tantrums when children really don't need to be restrained could condition them to distrust their own ability to handle anger or control their own temper.

Another reason why parents should avoid physically restraining children during tantrums, unless necessary, is because it constitutes an escalation of the conflict by the parents into a physical confrontation level. This always has the real potential of causing the children to counter-react physically towards the parents, initiating an actual physical power struggle that lasts until the children's tantrums subside. Anything that potentially emboldens or provokes children to react physically towards parents should not be undertaken lightly.

Parents can actually elicit Type-Two Tantrums by giving unthinking, or un-empathetic responses to children's original requests or demands that are manipulative from the first syllable. Conversely, parents can potentially thwart pre-tantrum manipulation, simply by getting into empathy mode immediately.

For example, say your child tries to manipulate you on the way home by asking the bogus question, "Remember you told me I could go to Jimmy's house after playschool?" It's probably best for you to *not* respond to such a question with the truthful yet fight-provoking words, "Uh, no, I didn't tell you that."

You could, instead, go straight into giving anticipatory empathy before the child is able to say another manipulative word—while still gently calling him on the lie. You could say: "I'm sorry honey. No, I was not at all aware that you wanted to go to Jimmy's house after school. I'm pretty sure I didn't say you could because today Grandma's coming over, and you didn't finish cleaning your room last night. You promised to finish cleaning it today, remember? But after you get your room done you can phone Jimmy to see if you can go over tomorrow."

You could be even more direct about discussing the manipulation yet still not be confrontational. Either at the beginning of the interaction or sometime later you could use the "I" statements, "I don't like it when you try to trick me into letting you play at Jimmy's. I'd rather you just ask me and then let me decide."

If you make efforts to give empathy to the manipulative child, but he still starts winding up to a tantrum, you could easily continue giving more empathy: "I'm sorry you're not happy. I can see you really want to spend time with

Jimmy. You really have fun with him, don't you? As soon as your room is clean, I'll let you phone him and ask if you can go over tomorrow." If the escalation continues, you could indicate to the child that you are about to withdraw the offer to play at Jimmy's the next day.

If this child is heavily into manipulating by tantrums, he probably wouldn't even let you get all of the empathy expressed before escalating straight into a tantrum. However, you are staying In Charge and not giving in to his manipulative demands. If the child escalates to a full-blown tantrum while you are driving, you could declare a loss of privilege for the tantrum behavior, pull off the road if necessary and possible, and even step out of the car while the child finishes screaming. I would advise stepping out of the car if it felt safe and like more of a Reset behavior than staying in the car. Or you could use ear plugs while staying in the car. For me, it would feel like more of a Reset to get out of the car and not have to listen to the screaming at such a painfully close range.

That's everything you need to know in order to prevent and eliminate temper tantrums in your child. It may take some time for you to become comfortable with all of the concepts and to learn to put them into practice. Once your child has learned to trust that your new responses are around to stay, you should no longer have to be supermindful of the tantrum triggers such as hunger, tiredness, and frustration. Those situations should stop triggering the tantrums because the new relationship dynamics should function as a safety catch.

However, you may not see a big difference in your child's behavior right away, and especially so if you've been dealing with Type-Two Tantrums for a number of years. In fact, if your child has been allowed to be In Charge for a number of years, he or she may initially put up a fair bit of resistance to relinquishing that control. If your child's intimidation tactics initially increase in response to your efforts to be more In Charge, or In Charge more of the time, try not to be discouraged. That could very well be a sign that you are on the right track.

Try to be analytical and not emotional about what is going on between you and your child. Document what occurs if that helps you analyze it. When you are able to consistently be and remain In Charge of your child in a firm and loving way and consistently give empathy for your child's anger, you should be able to eradicate any Type-Two Temper Tantrums.

If parents have been totally dependent on Time-outs as their only means of discipline and they now want to quit using them, they might choose to do so in a prepared way. It would be advisable for them to have a substitute plan thought out beforehand, perhaps with a handy list of fitting consequences for their children's standard offenses.

In this way, Time-out parents could pre-fill the potential void that quitting Time-outs would create. This would prevent bad-weather conditions of the brain—such as "brain fog" and "brain freeze"—while facing unfamiliar and important consequence decisions in front of children who are capable of intimidation. With this kind of preparation, I wouldn't anticipate any hazards from quitting the use of Time-outs with most children.

One exception might be with children who have had a habit of controlling parents with aggressive behavior. Another might be with children who have mental, emotional, or other disturbances. Such conditions could possibly contribute to a violent, conniving, or otherwise manipulative reaction to any major or abrupt changes in parenting practices.

Aside from these types of potential risks, I think Time-outs can be safely thrown out without any negative side effects. I would anticipate that most (if not all) parents who successfully transition from using Time-outs to giving natural, logical, and fitting consequences will very much feel like throwing a party and inviting their closest supporters to help them celebrate. In my opinion, this would be an extremely good premise for a party: *"No more* Time-outs*! Yeeeeeh haaaaah! Let's celebrate!"*

Perhaps you feel that you've adequately learned to apply the concepts I've presented, yet you haven't in a reasonable amount of time eliminated temper tantrums in your child. In such a case, I would recommend that you ask a trusted, concepts-familiar friend or relative to observe your application of them and give you some feedback. Or you could try to catch the beginnings of some of your child's tantrum episodes on a tape recorder or camcorder and then afterwards try to analyze what happened. If none of this reveals empathy, respect, or In Charge failings on your part, and you are still concerned with a lack of improvement, you might want to take your child to a physician or mental health professional to see if something else is possibly going on.

Parenting is a very difficult job. Unlike most others, it's a job of guesswork. Every child is unique. Everyone is constantly evolving and learning. No matter how much experience or time parents have had on the job, at any given moment it's impossible for them to be one hundred percent sure of making the right move. Plus, there is such a variety in parenting styles and techniques from which to choose that it often takes years of dedicated analytical parenting before people are able to strike their own balance.

A helpful tool for ascertaining where one should stand on any particular parenting or family issue is to try to step back from the situation and respectfully consider and weigh the needs of everyone involved. Also helpful is the ability to easily differentiate between higher-priority needs and lesser-priority wants. (For example, perhaps new clothing is a need, but new designer clothing is a want.)

It's important, also, to be aware of when wants transform into needs. Take, for instance, a mother who has neglected self-care to the point that her sustained mental health is in question. She may suddenly become acutely aware that locking herself in the bathroom and declaring her unavailability is not going to cut it this time. She may realize that a movie night out (which is normally only a want) suddenly has become an urgent need for her. Those kinds of prioritizing and awareness skills are really helpful for parents. However, no matter how many skills a parent acquires, parenting is always a very challenging job for those who care about doing the best they can at it.

I wish you great success in all aspects of your parenting endeavors and especially in being firm, loving, and In Charge, with ample empathy.

I invite any of my readers who would like to submit comments to me to do so on the *Comments* page of my website, www.megamomswisdom.com. Also, I invite all parents who have successfully eliminated temper tantrums from their child's behavior or prevented them in the first place to join my ***Tantrum-Free Club.***™ As the club grows in size, it could give lots of hope to suffering parents, encouraging them to reject the myth of tantrum inevitability and to correctly view tantrums as optional. I encourage you to share your success and help me help other parents to opt in to the tantrum-free lifestyle.

This book is also available as an eBook at
www.megamomswisdom.com

Chapter Twelve Summary: Application of the Principles

- The cause of Type-Two Temper Tantrums is a combination of the lack of a timely, caring, and empathetic response from the parent to the initial anger, plus some form of the parent not being adequately or consistently In Charge.

- The practice of quickly giving empathy for pre-tantrum anger is just as important in preventing Type-Two Tantrums as Type-Ones. Children who have learned to resort to manipulation when angry are certainly as needing and deserving of empathy for their anger as anyone else is.

- Besides giving empathy, how should parents of Type-Two Tantrum throwers react to the tantrums until they cease to occur? The first step should be for the parents to try to change the overall relationship dynamics by consistently being In Charge in a firm and loving way.

- Allowing a child to scream in public until voluntarily finished permits the child to show disrespect to others, does not properly prepare the child for the realities of functioning in school or any other public venue, and leaves the child's Unset action unchallenged.

- It's important that parents find firm and loving ways to push the Reset button as soon as possible after their children have hit the Unset button.

- It may take some time for you to become comfortable with these tantrum-prevention and tantrum-elimination concepts and learn to put them into practice.

- You may not see a difference in your child's behavior right away, and especially so if you've been dealing with Type-Two Tantrums for years. Eradicating Type-Two Tantrums may take considerably more time than it does to eliminate Type-One Tantrums.

- Parenting is always a very challenging job for those who care about doing it the best they can. Unlike many other jobs, parenting is a job of guesswork.

- Readers can submit comments to me on the *Comments* page of my website, www.megamomswisdom.com.

- I invite all parents who have successfully eliminated temper tantrums from their child's behavior or prevented them in the first place to join my *Tantrum-Free Club.*™ As the club grows in size, it could give lots of hope to suffering parents, encouraging them to reject the myth of tantrum inevitability and to correctly view tantrums as optional. I encourage you to share your success and help me help other parents to opt in to the tantrum-free lifestyle.

Epilogue

Like virtually all parents, my biggest dream was to raise happy, healthy, loving, functional children into happy, healthy, loving, functional adults. My only real personal difference from the norm was that my dream involved a larger-than-average number of children. Like multitudes of other women, though, I gradually realized over the years how complicated my dream had become by the negatives my parenting partners brought into the picture.

I had almost no assertiveness skills in the beginning and was mostly unable to withstand the pressures and manipulations I was subjected to in my first marriage. Not knowing how bad things actually were for my children as I struggled through that marriage, I steadfastly honored my early childhood vow to never divorce and subject my children to growing up without a father—as I had experienced. But ultimately my children suffered far worse because of my choice to stay in that marriage beyond the first few years. Sadly, countless other families, large and small, have suffered the same dynamics.

Additional, different parenting complications came with my second and third marriages—which I ended much more quickly—but still not quickly enough. My children and I have suffered many egregious situations, including a consistent lack of very basic financial resources. I did much to compensate financially for the large family size. I was highly productive and I worked sixteen hour days seven days a week for decades; however, my work-till-I-dropped-every-day lifestyle wasn't enough to compensate for my partners' lack of effort to provide. A psychologist who was working with me in dealing with some family fallout once said, "Leanna, every problem you have could be fixed with money." I agreed with her. That has been the story of my parenting life.

I wish I could have protected my children better. I wish I had been less naïve, less trusting of people who didn't deserve my trust, less long-suffering, and less unknowing about the dangers of being targeted and conned. I wish I had known enough back in the beginning to be selective in a marriage partner. (I actually thought that whichever person you fell in love with was automatically the "right" marriage partner for you.) I also wish I had made far fewer parenting mistakes.

Even if I'd had a really good parenting partner throughout, however, I'd have still made mistakes. We all do. But I've always tried to acknowledge and learn from my mistakes. I've typically been one to admit my own guilt to a fault—and long ago I even assumed more than my own guilt. In the fifties my mother could bring me to guilty sobs simply by summoning me with her index finger and saying sternly, "I have a bone to pick with you." It wasn't until the mid-seventies, however, that I suddenly realized how readily and automatically I assumed guilt that wasn't legitimately mine—just because my husband's finger was manipulatively pointed at me. From that moment on I determined to no longer accept guilt—unless, upon self-assessment, I decided it was mine to accept.

I have always done my utmost to be the best parent I could be in my circumstances, but my efforts were not enough to compensate for the harm caused to my children. Part of my ongoing difficulty is that my kids have not always understood or believed the circumstances I was dealing with. Some things are not appropriate to be explained to children, and some things can't be believed by them even years later because of lies they have been told and manipulations they have been subjected to.

One of the counselors who worked with our family after my first divorce explained a puzzling thing to me. He said that very often children in situations such as ours direct their anger and hatred much more towards the functional and stable parent for not protecting them—even if the need for protection was unknown—than towards the offending parent. He said children somehow sense that their anger and hatred can be more safely directed at the functional parent who will continue loving them no matter how viciously the children attack.

I accessed all the help I could possibly get and more help than my children would accept in trying to assist them in healing from their issues. Many times they were too young and not emotionally mature enough to take advantage of the available help, as is common for children in their circumstances. Consequently, a number of my grown children are still struggling today because of the original harm that was done, as well as its domino effects. However, I still hold out hope for continued healing as those who still need more become ready to work for it. I'm open, as I have been in the past, to honestly discuss the issues and help in any way I can.

I have been intensely saddened by the unnecessary pain that has been inflicted upon my children. I'm also saddened that some of them are still lost in that pain. We all have to heal from at least minimal childhood emotional neglect. No two parents—even exemplary ones—can possibly meet every emotional need of even a single child. This is because parents can't read minds and children don't know how to adequately communicate their emotional needs. We all need to heal from something in our upbringing. And the healing always requires effort.

Despite the outcome of my family's suffering, and maybe even to some degree because of it, I hope that the things I've learned can be of help to others.